# Kind Words

"What a fantastic, thought-provoking read! Jay explores 'busyness' and provides strategies for optimising a hectic lifestyle. By blending neuroscience with her own experiences, she offers a distinctive guide for navigating the busy world we inhabit! Bravo Jay".

—**Jasbir Sidhu**
Past President, UK Nuclear Institute

"A masterful guide to thriving rather than surviving in today's hectic work landscape. Through relatable scenarios and neuroscience-backed solutions, Jay makes complex topics more easily accessible and actionable for even the busiest individuals".

—**Anne Rey**
Director of Global Talent, Havas

"Jay's unique strength lies in providing a toolbox of tangible techniques from her interdisciplinary expertise in high-pressure environments. A must-read for those seeking proven strategies to cultivate unshakable composure and unlock their full potential".

—**Molly Dockree**
Senior Financial Analyst, Amazon

"This book is a survival manual offering immediately actionable strategies to navigate the complexities of modern life and relationships. With Jay's wisdom, it's like having your own brilliant neuroscientist strategist to guide you through today's pressurised world".

—**Marie Broad**
Corporate Social Responsibility, BDO LLP

"This book is for all who seek inspiration and expertise on personal development, managing through uncertainty, and building your leadership skills. Jay's book is like a long, thought-provoking session offering practical strategies to successfully manage today's realities".

—**Justyna Bielewicz**
International Brand & Comms Manager, Solventum

"Jay's book offers straightforward explanations from her extensive experience and passionate research, providing confidence to try new approaches. Her engaging style turns intimidating topics into practical tools for enhancing personal and professional relationships and managing everyday challenges".

**—Alison Forde**
Assistant Vice President, UBS

Brain
# Tools for the
Busy

# Brain Tools for the Busy

## Building Resilience Through Neuroscience and Eastern Wisdom

Jay Rai

WILEY

This edition first published 2025

© 2025, Jay Rai

*Registered Office(s)*

John Wiley & Sons, Inc., 111 River Street, Hoboken, NJ 07030, USA

John Wiley & Sons Ltd, The Atrium, Southern Gate, Chichester, West Sussex, PO19 8SQ, UK

John Wiley & Sons Singapore Pte. Ltd, 134 Jurong Gateway Road, #04-307H, Singapore 600134

For details of our global editorial offices, customer services, and more information about Wiley products visit us at www.wiley.com.

The manufacturer's authorized representative according to the EU General Product Safety Regulation is Wiley-VCH GmbH, Boschstr. 12, 69469 Weinheim, Germany, e-mail: Product_Safety@wiley.com.

Wiley also publishes its books in a variety of electronic formats and by print-on-demand. Some content that appears in standard print versions of this book may not be available in other formats.

*Library of Congress Cataloging-in-Publication Data:*

Print LCCN 2024923403

ISBN: 9781394218417 (Hardback)

ISBN: 9781394218431 (ePDF)

ISBN: 9781394218424 (ePUb)

Cover Design: Wiley

Cover Art: © 3d_kot/Adobe Stock Photos

Printed and bound by CPI Group (UK) Ltd, Croydon CR0 4YY

C9781394218417_070125

The manufacturer's authorized representative according to the EU General Product Safety Regulation is Wiley-VCH GmbH, Boschstr. 12, 69469 Weinheim, Germany, e-mail: Product_Safety@wiley.com.

*To you, dear reader, may you discover insightful strategies and practical wisdom within these pages.*

# Contents

# Acknowledgements

This book wouldn't have come to life without some incredible people. To my dearest friend Elora Das, your saintly patience and dedication helped make this dream a reality. I couldn't have done it without you. To Anna Esposito for tirelessly going through my drafts until I finally found my voice—your contribution has been incredibly generous.

A special shoutout to my little motivator and nephew Taran, whose charming impatience "When can I buy your book, Auntie?" became the anthem of my perseverance.

I am immensely grateful to the Wiley team, particularly Annie Knight, my brilliant editor, who first discovered my musings among the sea of professionals on LinkedIn. Thank you for believing in me and knowing the right words to lift my spirits and sharpen my resolve. Alice Hadaway for your endless perseverance in finding the perfect look for this book; and to Gus Miklos, the master of tone and flow, thank you for weaving your magic into these pages.

To everyone who pitched in—whether with a kind comment, a hug, or a shove—I appreciate you.

And, of course, a heartfelt thank you to you, the reader, for taking time out of your busy schedule to explore *Brain Tools for the Busy*. I hope it offers you the clever insights you seek and nudges you closer to being your most authentic self each day.

# About the Author

**Jay Rai (MSc)** is a specialist in the field of Neuroscience and Psychology of Mental Health. She is known for her innovative approach that blends neuroscience, psychology, and Eastern mindfulness practices. Jay's focus is on helping others live authentically, a mission that stems from her own transition from the high-paced world of investment management to her true calling in mental health, which is a testament to her commitment to making a genuine difference.

At the core of Jay's methodology is her robust experience, honed at the Priory Clinic—one of the United Kingdom's largest mental health addiction centres. Here, she refined her skills, gaining deep insights into the complexities of mental well-being. Jay is also a member of the British Neuroscience Association and Forbes Coaches Council.

Beyond her consultancy, Jay is a sought-after speaker, sharing her insights at leading global organisations, including Google and Amazon. Her talks resonate with professionals eager to boost their mental resilience and growth while managing their busy lives.

Jay's work centres around practical and impactful change. Her ability to weave together neuroscience with time-honoured psychotherapeutic and mindfulness techniques makes her a unique voice in the field.

Please direct questions to: jay@jayrai.com

# Preface

In my years working in the investment management industry, I constantly sought tools to help me manage the many responsibilities I juggled without slowing me down. The fast-paced nature of the job demanded efficiency and precision, pushing me to find ways to manage everything (including my sanity). This drive was not only a professional need but also a personal quest.

As I transitioned into my clinical work, I noticed that many professional clients also faced similar challenges. They needed solutions to streamline their lives, allowing them to concentrate on what truly mattered. This commonality between my two career paths revealed a universal need for effective tools that empower individuals to manage their lives without compromise.

When Wiley presented me with the opportunity to author this book, I immediately had a clear vision of the path I wanted to take. Drawing from my personal experiences and the insights gained from my clients, representing various industries and backgrounds, this book provides readers with practical strategies that I have found invaluable. By sharing these resources, I hope others will feel better equipped to navigate their busy days with greater ease and confidence.

# Introduction

Welcome to a journey that is anything but a simple regurgitation of the same worn-out advice, or an offering of inspirational platitudes. Instead, you're invited to an engaging exploration of the chaos and rush that characterises our lives—you know, that constant desire to do more, be more, and accomplish more.

I turned to the self-help sections in my own search for sanity but found that a lot of the guidance only seemed to heighten my stress rather than alleviate it. Consider the well-meaning suggestion to "carve out time for yourself". It sounds wonderful in theory. In reality, it often felt like yet another chore on my unfinished agenda, triggering feelings of guilt rather than personal development. What I truly needed were approaches that I could seamlessly fit into my routine, not throw it into disarray.

This book was written as a result of this realisation. Preaching from an ivory tower is not the point. Instead, it's about standing by your side and offering up my own experiences, insights, and hard-won wisdom. I understand what it's like to battle in the corporate trenches where predictability doesn't exist, so if phrases like "strive for a balanced work–life" make you roll your eyes, you're in the perfect place. In pursuit of real answers, my scepticism led me into the intriguing fields of neuroscience and mental health psychology in search of practical solutions that actually work.

My professional journey also took me through the intense environments of drug and trauma rehabilitation centres. Just in case you're wondering what it's like, well, imagine being in a pressure cooker every day, confronting intense and emotionally draining situations head-on. In this environment the feelings of anger, anxiety, and intense suffering aren't abstract concepts; they're as real as the air we breathe.

However, it was inside these walls that I stumbled upon an unexpected discovery. I didn't weaken under the pressure but became stronger. Rather than feeling depleted by the intensity, I developed a renewed sense of energy. Working in this turbulent and demanding setting became my teacher, guiding me to create techniques that not only strengthened my own resilience but also refined my coaching abilities. These transformations significantly influenced how I tackled my work, turning high-pressure strategies into effective coaching tools.

My curiosity in applying these methods in business ultimately resulted in exciting collaborations with companies like Google and Amazon, focusing on enhancing mental resilience.

Think of this book as a culmination of all those experiences. It's far from your typical resilience guide; au contraire. It is a detailed manual for thriving in today's demanding world. Meticulously curated, it provides techniques to energise you and conquer daily challenges. You'll learn to increase productivity through innovative and enjoyable methods, establish healthy boundaries, handle conflict skilfully, control stress and anxiety with no-nonsense strategies, transform negative thoughts, and develop strong emotional intelligence and self-assurance along the way. I've stripped away the filler and given you clear and actionable strategies that you can easily incorporate into your daily schedule. These strategies will help strengthen mental fortitude while respecting your time and intellect.

Over the years, I found myself pulled in by the allure of four different worlds: psychology, philosophy, psychotherapy, and the intriguing field of neuroscience. Each one had its own unique charm. Psychology with its roadmap on how our brains tick, philosophy inviting deep thinking and questioning what's real. Psychotherapy the wise friend giving solid advice and neuroscience the cutting-edge explorer of the brain's hidden secrets.

That's exactly the reason why I've incorporated aspects from all four fields into this book. By combining the perspectives of psychology, the questions of philosophy, the practical methods of psychotherapy, and the innovative findings of neuroscience, you can develop a richer, more detailed insight into human nature. This promises to offer practical tools for navigating life with more clarity, intention, and satisfaction.

Flexibility is a key theme in this guide. Whether you're zeroing in on a specific challenge or exploring the entire spectrum of strategies, the power rests firmly in your hands. The visual aids included are not just for decoration; capturing a screenshot can provide a quick and handy reminder whenever you need it. Ultimately, this book serves as your roadmap to becoming a stronger, more resilient version of yourself.

# 1

# The Bright Side of Busy

Remember when "busy" was just… busy? Now, it seems like we've all hit the accelerator from "super busy" straight to "outright manic". And yet, despite this, there remains an ironic abundance of time dedicated to vocalising our sense of overwhelm. It's as though our collective narrative has been hijacked, convincing us that this non-stop pace blurs our focus, amps up our anxiety, and chips away at our overall happiness. The prevailing wisdom screams at us from all corners: slow down, unplug, seek tranquillity. Busyness, it seems, has been cast as the villain in our modern-day story, an adversary we're encouraged to out-manoeuvre at every turn.

Now, allow me to offer a viewpoint that suggests a new way to look at your busy life. What if instead of seeing busyness as the enemy, you see it as a misunderstood ally? From this perspective, I would like to welcome you to join me on a journey—a road less travelled as it were—where you get to reconsider the essence of living a life filled to the brim with responsibilities.

The core of this discussion is the concept of *intentional busyness*. This isn't an ode to cramming every possible task into your calendar, or even romanticising the hustle. No, this is about consciously choosing to engage with your busy life deliberately, with eyes wide open, and keeping your values and priorities in sharp focus. I'm not advocating for squeezing more into the finite hours of your days; instead, the aim is to infuse real meaning, passion, and connection into the time you have. This approach urges you to focus on enriching the aspects of your life that truly resonate with you and help you grow in the directions you aspire to.

Just in case you were wondering, this investigation into busyness isn't just a product of my whimsical musings. We are standing on pretty solid ground here backed by robust evidence, tried and true therapeutic methods, and the profound philosophical inquiries that have intrigued great thinkers for generations. Together, we'll uncover how to breathe fresh energy into your everyday schedules.

When you start to challenge the narrative of being "too busy", you're not just going against the norm of it just being a fast track to burnout; you're reclaiming your power by creating space to reimagine busyness as a chance for personal growth rather than a source of mere exhaustion.

## Reimagining Busyness

I often compare being overly busy to that one friend who never quite seems to take the hint. They show up uninvited, dominate your time, and always linger. Just like that friend, busyness also tends to chat with you incessantly and linger around when all you crave is a moment of peace. If you're anything like me, sometimes life just feels like an endless loop: finish one task and just when you're ready to relax—hey, voilà—two more tasks pop up to take its place. It's as if our brains are hardwired to engage with this never-ending game of planning and problem-solving, to the point where even our dreams aren't safe from turning into protracted to-do lists.

But what if you stopped viewing this continual activity as an enemy? What if, rather than letting it drain you, you could tap into its power? Think of it as consciously choosing your battles, or as I like to call it, choosing intentional busyness. It's about going about your daily activities but on your own terms. This means steering the busyness, not just being dragged along by it and perhaps even finding a sprinkle of excitement in the process.

But, before we get too ahead of ourselves, there's an important caveat to consider. Even though I support the benefits of intentional busyness, it's important to acknowledge the drawbacks of constantly being busy. Being productively occupied isn't the same as using busyness as a way to put off solving more important issues. I've certainly fallen prey to this trap myself, confusing motion for progress and letting the "busy" buzz overpower my inner voice telling me to attend to personal matters. It's an alluring trap that uses the hustle as a hiding place.

Intentional busyness is not about ignoring these challenges. Actually, quite the opposite is true. It pushes you to confront them directly, honestly, and sincerely. Rather than taking shortcuts, it's about intentionally travelling through your busy days to achieve genuine progress and personal satisfaction.

## A Journey from Busy to Intentional

Have you ever caught yourself thinking that perhaps all this busyness isn't just a laundry list of things to get done? It's almost like holding up a mirror. It can show you your deepest fears, your wildest hopes, and how you choose to face the day ahead. I regularly meet people in my clinic who treat their work as a lifeboat. They devote all of their valuable energy to being busy, utilising their hectic schedules as a smoke screen against the vulnerability that comes with confronting their genuine feelings.

And I am no exception. I recall one particular evening that was, like so many of my evenings, anything but relaxing. As usual, I had every intention of taking it easy, but before long, I found myself tethered to my desk once more. Here I was ostensibly free, but somehow I'd drifted back to my all-too-familiar perch. As I stared absentmindedly at my computer screen, a slow realisation began to creep up on me. I wasn't simply caught up in constant busyness; I was also actively contributing to it. It's a situation many of us find embarrassingly familiar, right?

This is where the idea of intentional busyness first took shape. Several books I'd read over the years kept pointing to this concept but it never quite clicked until now. Cal Newport's *Deep Work*

(Grand Central Publishing, 2016)[1] in particular highlights the importance of focused, meaningful activity over busy work. It's a departure from the autopilot mode you're all too familiar with. Rather than being ruled by your busyness, you take the reins. You choose to consciously immerse yourself in your dynamic life, converting the kinetic energy of busyness into a force for both personal and professional growth, not just a series of tasks to be checked off.

In the following sections, I will guide you through practically applying this way of thinking. We will explore methods to not only deal with everyday challenges but also turn them to your advantage. However, let's first consider the positive changes that can result from embracing an intentionally busy mindset.

## The Benefits of Being Busy

Whenever you think about your busy schedule it's all too common to focus on the stress and pressure it brings, and understandably so. However, there is a silver lining to the hustle and bustle that often goes unnoticed. This conversation isn't about learning anything new that exists outside of yourself, but tapping into your inner potential through keeping yourself intentionally busy. Let's now explore three key benefits of adopting this mindset: sharpening your focus, sparking your creativity, and aligning with your natural rhythm. Along the way, you'll also learn more about the engine that powers your ability to adapt while leading a busy life.

### Sharpening Your Focus

We're living in an era where silence is golden but increasingly rare. Every day we are bombarded with pings and alert notifications, all clamouring for our attention. Surprisingly, this busy environment offers a chance to practise intentional busyness, directing our focus to make our time meaningful.

By filtering out daily distractions, and immersing your attention fully into tasks at hand, you can enhance your brain's ability to concentrate. Both ancient philosophies and contemporary studies alike

---

[1] Newport, Cal. Deep Work: Rules for Focused Success in a Distracted World. Grand Central Publishing, 2016.

suggest that honing your focus, in the midst of all the madness, is kind of like possessing a superpower. In essence, being busy is more than just getting things done; it's about leveraging your hectic schedules to improve your concentration and mental health.

Interestingly, your bodies also love it when you're "dialled in". Engage deeply with what you do, and your brain thanks you by dishing out dopamine and endorphins, or what I affectionately call our biochemical cheerleaders. These natural feel-good chemicals boost your mood, motivation, and fuel your drive to keep going.[2]

But the benefits of sharpening your focus also extend far beyond your work. It's about deeply engaging with whatever, or whomever, requires your present moment's attention. So, this could mean investing yourself more wholly in your personal relationships, hobbies, or nurturing stronger connections.

This shift in viewpoint can greatly boost your confidence because it reinforces your capacity to manage multiple elements of your life effectively. As you start to see yourself successfully managing activities and deepening connections, you build a sense of competence and self-assurance. This encourages you to consider larger obstacles not as hurdles but as chances for growth.

Furthermore, this combination of focused effort and increased confidence paves the way for creativity. Surprisingly, contrary to what one might expect, the efficiency and clarity gained from such focus act as catalysts for innovative thinking. With the distractions managed and chaos under control, your mind can wander into new territories, uncover new ideas, and make strides in creativity.[3]

### Finding Creativity in the Chaos

When we dream about unleashing our creative energy, we often envision tranquil, undisturbed havens apart from life's usual chaos and distractions. However, through my own journey, I've discovered an unexpected

---

[2] Breuning, L.G. (2016). *Habits of a Happy Brain*. Avon, MA: Adams Media. Available at: https://workmindfulness.com/wp-content/uploads/2017/11/Loretta-Graziano-Breuning-Habits-of-a-Happy-Brain-Adams-Media-2016.pdf.

[3] Zedelius, C.M. and Schooler, J.W. (2015). Mind wandering 'Ahas' versus mindful reasoning: Alternative routes to creative solutions. *Frontiers in Psychology* 6: 834. Available at: https://doi.org/10.3389/fpsyg.2015.00834.

reality: the same messiness and demands of daily life, even with its inherent instability, may actually be the unlikely muse we've been overlooking.

Sounds paradoxical, doesn't it? Let me walk you through it. Imagine yourself in the thick of a particularly frenzied week: deadlines are breathing down your neck, family schedules clashing, and personal tasks piling up in the background. In these moments of chaos, something rather curious happens. Your mind begins to wander and innovate. It begins connecting dots and stitching together ideas in ways that just don't happen during calmer times.

Let's take a quick little detour into the world of neuroscience to understand why this happens. Your brain thrives when fed a diet of varied inputs and challenges. Immersing yourself in diverse situations can prime your brain for creative breakthroughs, making you better at conjuring up innovative ideas.[4] Think of a chef in a busy kitchen, experimenting with all sorts of exotic and unusual ingredients. Amidst the noise and heat, they can create dishes that no cookbook could have ever dreamed up. This analogy also extends to your life; driven by the pace of your busy days, your mind blends experiences and insights that lead you to explore new perspectives and solutions.

When you realise that it is the very unyielding daily push and pull of life that can actually fuel creative thinking, you can learn to work with it rather than resist it. It's under the pressure of tight deadlines that you're driven to find innovative solutions. Research shows that pressure can enhance creativity by pushing our brains to explore unconventional paths. In this rush, your mind becomes finely tuned and ready to catch and mould those fleeting moments of inspiration into meaningful ideas.

But here's where it gets even better. This hectic juggling act also opens you up to collaboration. Whether that is brainstorming in team meetings, engaging in imaginative play with kids, or bouncing ideas off friends—all these collective melding of minds create a rich mix of thoughts. It's in these exchanges that creativity truly blossoms, sparking broader communal innovation.

---

[4] Abraham, A. (2013). The promises and perils of the neuroscience of creativity. *Frontiers in Human Neuroscience* 7: 246. Available at: https://www.frontiersin.org/articles/10.3389/fnhum.2013.00246/full.

### Finding Rhythm in the Rush

Have you ever experienced that feeling of being swamped only to pause and contemplate if there's a purpose to life beyond routine? It's as if we're all connected to this rhythm, where our actions either harmonise with or disrupt the natural order of the universe. This concept has fascinated people for ages, compelling us to seek out significance and purpose in our lives that transcend the aspects of our existence.

If you really do stop and think about it, every choice you make, regardless of its size, plays a role in shaping your life. This viewpoint has the potential to change your perception of your habits. The great German philosopher Friedrich Nietzsche, in *Twilight of the Idols* (1889),[5] famously wrote: "Without music, life would be a mistake". I feel he may have also been hinting at finding harmony in our everyday lives, despite its challenges, and discovering a melody in the mundane moments.

I remember one particular afternoon, wandering through an art gallery in my twenties. It was so quiet you could hear your own heartbeat. It's as if the silence made each piece of art pulse with its own rhythm. One painting in particular caught my eye. It looked pretty crazy and chaotic at first, but the more I stared at it the more I found it to reveal a pattern. The only way I can think to explain it was that I could begin to see how the colours and shapes merged together, each bold stroke contributing to the overall masterpiece.

As I've reflected on this experience over the years, it has taught me that even when life feels chaotic, if you really tune in, there's a rhythm to it all. Your days and decisions are also like brushstrokes on life's canvas, adding up to something bigger and more beautiful. So, maybe the trick is to learn to listen to your own pulse and find your own beat. By doing that, you might just see the bigger picture of your life, realising the masterpiece you're collectively painting—one day and one decision at a time.

Let's now turn our attention to the underlying engine that powers our adaptability and creative surges.

---

[5] Nietzsche, Friedrich. 1889. *Twilight of the Idols.*

## The Busy Path to a More Adaptable Brain

Long gone are the days when we believed our minds were set in stone after childhood. Nowadays, I think we all understand that the brain has the capacity to grow and adapt over time, and that's all thanks to a concept known as neuroplasticity. This concept highlights our ability to build resilience through adjusting to new circumstances, showing us that we are constantly evolving. One of my clients aptly made a comparison describing our brain as a live document; continuously undergoing revisions and updates and always in a state of flux.

Leading a busy life makes neuroplasticity even more important. Because a busy routine not only tests our limits, it strengthens our brain. Each difficulty solved, multitask managed, or new ability gained fortifies the brain, making it more agile and capable.

But here's where it gets even more interesting. It's not just about you getting smarter or more skilled. It deeply affects how you connect with others. Diving into deep conversations, truly listening, and showing support aren't just nice things to do; they're like a gym session for your brain, building up those neural connections that pump up your emotional intelligence and help forge deeper bonds with the people around you.

So, what's the takeaway? Instead of seeing a busy schedule as a burden, see it as an opportunity for intentional action. Because engaging deliberately in complex challenges and meaningful exchanges leverages the neuroplasticity of your brain, turning what could be overwhelming into a mechanism for personal growth.

The next two chapters delve further into how you can not only guard your energy, but use your busyness to manage your energy in positive ways.

# Energise and Conquer

This section focuses on empowering you to take charge of your energy levels and optimise your daily routine for peak performance and wellness. You will learn straightforward strategies to protect and reinvigorate your energy by viewing it as an asset that requires thoughtful handling.

Chapter 2 introduces the benefit of thinking of yourself as a battery, and in doing so, you will discover how to pinpoint what depletes your energy and apply techniques to recharge yourself. The focus is on sustaining performance by protecting your energy reservoirs and ensuring you remain energised throughout the day. It offers practical steps to help you efficiently manage your energy levels.

In Chapter 3, you will learn a playful yet strategic approach to aligning your daily responsibilities with your body's natural rhythms. The concept of an "Energy Playlist" is introduced, to assist you in structuring your day based on your pace. By syncing tasks with your energy highs and lows, you'll learn how to make the most of your day by ensuring your efforts are as efficient as possible.

Throughout this section, you'll gain valuable suggestions on handling your energy and planning your day to hit your targets. The goal is to provide you with resources that harness your body's natural cycles, enabling you to reach your destination with a sense of determination and efficiency.

# 2

# Power Protect: Guard Your Energy Like a Pro

**Figure 2.1   Protect Your Energy**

**When to Use.**   For moments when your body's present, your mind's checked out, and your spirit is AWOL, leaving you totally drained.

This chapter aims to assist you in protecting your energy like never before. This four-step approach emphasises the significance of your energy and offers advice on how to safeguard it, similar to how you would shield a flame from the wind to ensure it continues to burn brightly.

Imagine, if you will, energy not just as a utility that powers your phone or lights up your room, but as the very force propelling every thought, igniting every burst of laughter, motivating every step forward, and fuelling every aspiration. By understanding your energy in this way, the feeling of fatigue then becomes not just a physical need for caffeine to jumpstart your day; it's a deeper sense of being burdened by even the simplest everyday tasks, rendering your dreams seemingly out of reach. When you fail to manage this crucial energy effectively, you may find yourself adrift and disconnected from what truly matters. Indeed, this perspective is not a mere flight of fancy. It mirrors your everyday reality, underscoring the critical role energy plays in your existence. This insight begs an essential question: How do you guard and optimise this vital force? The answer to this question began to unfold for me in an unexpected setting—while guiding individuals in rehab through their battles with substance abuse and trauma.

It was in these moments of profound human struggle that I stumbled upon a strategy that quickly became my lifeline: I've named it *Power Protect*. Initially, it emerged as a personal tool designed to manage the emotional toll of my work. Yet, the more I immersed myself in this concept, the more it evolved, transcending its original intent. It transformed into a comprehensive approach for not just getting by, but growing stronger in the thick of ups and downs. This realisation of its broader applicability was a watershed moment. It had an impact not just on my professional life but on all aspects of how I face life's challenges.

This epiphany was like turning on a light in a dark room. Instead of ignoring my energy, I turned it into something tangible—a rechargeable battery, indeed a concept so simple yet utterly transformative. I started to evaluate each thought, decision, action, and emotion in terms of their impact on my energy; were they charging me up or draining me? This new lens brought clarity and replaced the confusion between what replenished my energy and what sapped it. No longer was I a passive participant, at the mercy of external circumstances, blown about like a leaf in the wind. Instead, I had a way to actively manage and command my energy levels.

This knowledge is not a secret that I've kept hidden until now. I have shared this approach in countless corporate boardrooms and workshop settings, observing its remarkable influence in these professional landscapes. Many individuals have come to rely on the Power Protect method in managing both their personal and professional lives with greater poise and confidence.

Mastering the art of protecting your energy is, however, just one part of the equation. Equally important is understanding its dynamic nature: how it ebbs and flows within you.

## Understanding the Rise and Fall of Your Energy

You know those times when your brain seems to have hit a wall and just won't cooperate, and suddenly even the simplest tasks feel as complex as rocket science? This sensation isn't just a sign of a bad day. It's actually a common distress signal. A desperate message from our bodies saying, "Hey, we're running low on fuel here!" It clearly shows that our energy levels are dropping. Our brains, those incredible powerhouses, are the life of the party despite their compact size. They are also the most high-maintenance guests at the energy party, guzzling a staggering 20% of our body's energy.[1] This significant energy use is vital because it facilitates our thoughts, decisions, and emotions, ensuring the smooth sailing of our daily lives. Therefore, when we're blindsided by a wave of fatigue, it's really our brain hoisting up a white flag signalling its need for a time-out to refuel.

But our brains aren't just insatiable energy consumers; they're also masterful energy savers.[2] They draw from past experiences to predict future needs, much like how we automatically know to grab an umbrella at the sight of a grumpy sky. However, this drive for efficiency

[1] Magistretti, P.J. and Allaman, I. (2015). A cellular perspective on brain energy metabolism and functional imaging. *Neuron* 85(7): 883–901. Available at: https://www.cell.com/neuron/fulltext/S0896-6273(15)00259-7.
[2] Shulman, R.G., Rothman, D.L., Behar, K.L. et al. (2004). Energetic basis of brain activity: Implications for neuroimaging. *Trends in Neurosciences* 27(8): 489–495.

has its downsides, often causing us to prioritise saving energy over staying fully engaged.[3] Think about a day filled with meetings. As time passes you might find yourself going through the motions on autopilot, completing tasks mechanically with decreasing enthusiasm. While this strategy may keep mental fatigue at bay for a while, overdependence on it can spiral into a pervasive sense of weariness.[4] This isn't a reflection of incompetence or lack of drive but a clear sign of our brain's tendency to choose conservation over full-throttle engagement.

In the world of rehabilitation, where my resilience was tested daily against both physical and emotional tolls, the parallels to our everyday energy battles are strikingly evident. Just as in rehab, our daily lives are filled with moments that test our energy alignment. Those days when everything feels off-kilter, from the minor annoyance of spilt coffee to the frustration of forgetting a familiar name, underscore our struggle with energy misalignment. The sway of our energy levels casts a long shadow over our existence, influencing everything from our productivity to our mood swings. The encouraging part is that by being mindful and making an effort to manage our energy proactively, we can realign it and bring it back into a harmonious equilibrium.

Given the colossal energy demands of our brain and its clever ways to save energy, it's no surprise that we go through ups and downs in our mental vitality. This isn't a flaw but a built-in reminder that it's time to decelerate and recharge. It goes without saying that the impact of sleep quality, nutrition, mental health, and physical activity on our energy equilibrium is undeniable. But the secret to lasting energy and strength is paying attention to these signals. Adopting rejuvenating habits that align with our brain's natural rhythms and requirements.

Next up, I'll walk you through some practical steps for reinvigorating your energy while on the go. Because, at the end of the day, we all deserve to experience life fully charged one energised step at a time.

---

[3] Kurzban, R., Duckworth, A., Kable, J.W. et al. (2013). An opportunity cost model of subjective effort and task performance. *Behavioral and Brain Sciences* 36(6): 661–679. doi: 10.1017/S0140525X12003196.

[4] Boksem, M.A.S. and Tops, M. (2008). Mental fatigue: Costs and benefits. *Brain Research Reviews* 59(1): 125–139.

## Guide: Managing Your Energy

This section discusses in more detail the strategy of the Power Protect methods that are both simple and impactful. The main concept revolves around likening your energy to a battery. You will explore how your thoughts, decisions, behaviours, and emotions influence your energy levels. The objective of this four-step approach is to assist you in efficiently protecting your energy, helping you to shield the flame that is your personal power.

### *Step 1: Check Your Battery Level*

When you begin your day, it's important to gauge your energy levels like how you would glance at your phone's battery. In an ideal world, you'd wake up fully charged at 100% ready for whatever comes your way. But in reality, factors such as a bad night's sleep or getting stuck ruminating on problems might mean that you're kicking off the day at around 70%, 50%, or even lower.

Why does this matter? Identifying your starting energy level is the first key step to managing your energy. It essentially states, "Today, I'm beginning at 60%". This isn't a precursor to defeat; rather, it's about tailoring your day's ambitions to your current state. Operating with 60% energy? Then lining up tasks that consume roughly 60% of your energy reserves aligns perfectly with your capacity. It's a strategic move.

**Application.** You wake up already dreading the packed schedule awaiting you. And thanks to last night's unresolved argument replaying in your mind, you're not exactly jumping out of bed full of zest. Instead of forcing false positivity, pause for an honest assessment and acknowledge that today you're at 60%.

It might be a bit of a let-down to admit this, but this honesty is actually your secret weapon. It allows you to recalibrate your day's expectations—prioritising tasks that match your current energy levels. Opting to tackle the most critical 60% of your tasks suddenly turns a potentially daunting day into something far more manageable.

**Insight.** Success doesn't mean you need to be firing on all cylinders all the time. It's more about smartly managing the energy you've got and understanding that it's okay for your levels to fluctuate—some days you might feel like you're at 70% and other times you might be coasting at 40%. The trick is to select and accomplish tasks that align with your current energy level. Importantly, this approach isn't just about reaching for any low-hanging fruit; it's about strategically choosing the right ones for you. Think of aligning your tasks with your current energy as a target. Sure, hitting it every time might not be possible, but aiming for it is what counts. Plus, on those lower-energy days, completing tasks that match your energy level for the day is a win in itself.

### Step 2: Identify What Drains You

Let's face it, every single thing you do, big or small, can end up draining your energy. Whether it's making decisions, wrestling with your thoughts (the good, the bad, and the ugly), dealing with arguments, or simply working through your daily checklist, all of it chips away at your energy bit by bit.

Acknowledging this reality helps you understand that maintaining your energy isn't just about managing what you do. It's about pinpointing and addressing the habits that sap your strength.

**Application.**    Ah, it's Saturday again, your designated "get stuff done" day. Your laundry basket's overflowing, your kitchen's a disaster zone, and there's a grocery run that is as detailed as a military operation. And let's not forget the social obligations: coffee with a friend who's back in town, and a dinner you promised you wouldn't miss this time. Does this sound like a typical weekend?

Here's the thing: treating each activity as if it's another tab open in your brain's browser is a sure-fire way to deplete your mental energy fast. I used to be guilty of this; trying to juggle everything at once and wondering why I felt like a zombie by the afternoon. I now understand that it wasn't just the volume of tasks but my scattergun approach to them that left me drained.

So, I changed things up. To reduce the amount of time spent jumping between chores, I began grouping tasks to cut down on the run-around. But the real shift happened with my lunchtime coffee ritual. Instead of zoning out on WhatsApp or Instagram to avoid dreading the rest of the day's tasks, I chose to actually enjoy and savour my coffee, totally absorbed in the present moment. This was a deliberate choice to give my brain a chance to take a break from distracting activities, to reset and recharge. This brief detachment not only elevated my simple coffee break into a moment of intentional energy replenishment but led to clearer thinking and improved problem-solving when I returned to my tasks.

The result? On days when vitality coursed through me, I'd conquer my entire agenda. On the more subdued days, I addressed only what my reserves could handle. This practice, inspired by Eastern philosophy, emphasises the importance of balancing effort with available energy. It taught me the importance of aligning what I get done with how much energy I have, leading to a real sense of satisfaction when it all lines up.

**Insight.** Managing energy isn't optional; it's essential. Identify what drains your energy each day and devise a plan to address it without going bankrupt on your energy account. It's less about busting a gut to get through your entire to-do list and more about selecting which tasks to prioritise. And what about that coffee break? Make it count. Sometimes, it's the most productive thing you didn't know you needed.

Looking at it from a neuroscience perspective, this approach aligns with our brain's natural rhythm of energy expenditure and recovery. Your brain, just like every other organ, needs downtime to recover from periods of high intensity. By organising your days to match your true energy levels, and taking breaks that you genuinely enjoy, you're not fighting your brain's wiring—you're using it to your advantage, leading to improved focus and less mental tiredness.

### Step 3: Lighten Your Energy Load

Every worry, especially about things beyond your control, drains your brain battery power at warp speed. So, what's the move when you're staring down the barrel of a situation out of your control? Sink under the weight of dread, or meet it with a kind of charged-up resolve?

Whether you choose fear or excitement, they are essentially two sides of the same emotional coin. It truly comes down to perspective.

Seeing a challenge as a chance to shine rather than a nightmare scenario can significantly shift your energy flow. This mental flip transforms anxiety into a force more like adrenaline, gearing you up not just to cope but to excel. You've got a choice: let fear sap your energy or channel that tension into momentum towards your objectives.

**Application.**     Imagine you're on track with a project, and suddenly the deadline's on fast-forward. Initial reaction? Full-blown panic. But as you know, fretting won't extend your timeline, it'll just drain your energy faster.

Now, let's adjust that view with some practical reframing. Instead of viewing the situation as a panic-inducing mess, view it as an opportunity to showcase your ability to adapt and overcome. This moment isn't just another day; it's your time to shine. Perhaps ask yourself: "What would someone inspirational, like [insert the name of an inspirational figure you admire], do in this situation?" This question isn't just a thought exercise; it works because it taps into the mindset of success. Emulating the actions and attitudes of those you admire, such as their resilience or composure, offers you a blueprint to follow, guiding you with a clear path forward to push past stress and step into a state of productive readiness.

The next step is crucial. Instead of getting tangled up in the "what ifs", zoom in on what you can actually affect. Assess your time available and ask yourself: "What are the best moves I can make with the time I have?" This isn't about changing the deadline; it's about optimising your approach to meet it.

By channelling your energy in this way towards solution-seeking and asserting control, you effectively reclaim the reins. This mindset pivots you away from stress towards excited action, prepping you to confront that new deadline head-on, with a clear, action-ready attitude.

**Insight.**     The shift from fear to excitement isn't just motivational. It's supported by the groundbreaking research of Alison Wood Brooks at Harvard University. Her studies demonstrate that individuals who reinterpret their nervous energy as excitement do better in stressful situations, such as public speaking, than those who fixate on their anxiety.[5]

Adopting this strategy fundamentally alters your brain's reaction to stress, converting stress and anxiety into a chance for excitement while boosting resilience and productivity. Engaging in this mental shift on a regular basis not only saves energy but also improves your ability to tackle challenges effectively.

### Step 4: Power Up

We all know the drill: sleep powers us up like a charger, food acts as our power bank, and exercise gives us that extra boost. But what else keeps your battery from hitting red during the course of your day? It might be a quick temperature reset, stepping outside to experience a different temperature and invigorating yourself, grabbing coffee with a colleague, enjoying a family meal on Sunday, or zoning out to your favourite sitcom reruns in the evening. These moments are the sparks that keep your energy levels topped up.

However, recharging shouldn't just become another item on your endless to-do list. It's less about squeezing more into your day than deriving greater value from the things you already do. Savour those moments, laugh louder, and immerse fully; that's where the real energy comes from. Einstein had it right when he said, "Energy cannot be created or destroyed; it can only be changed from one form to another". We're talking about turning the simple stuff—like a conversation over coffee or getting lost in a book—into pure, actionable energy.

Whenever I fully engage in these kinds of uplifting experiences, I always take a moment to reflect on my feel-good emotions afterwards and tell my brain, "Hey that felt energising, let's create more moments like this". This practice not only reinforces the positive

---

[5] Brooks, A.W. (2014). Get excited: Reappraising pre-performance anxiety as excitement. *Journal of Experimental Psychology: General* 143(3): 1144–1158.

experiences but also encourages my brain to seek out and repeat these kinds of energy-boosting activities.

**Application.** Imagine you've trudged through another brutal week. You know the kind—where it was punctuated by tough decisions, strenuous dialogues with loved ones, or personal obstacles that pushed your resilience to its limits. You're not just tired; you feel like someone drained your battery and then some.

So, you promise yourself the weekend will be different. Maybe you'll binge that popular series, dive into a DIY project, or catch up with a friend. Suddenly, these simple acts become your recharge.

I've overlooked these moments too, not realising they were precisely what I needed. Recognising these activities as your personal chargers can significantly boost your satisfaction. And the best part? It doesn't require packing more into your schedule.

**Insight.** Choosing to recharge means filling your energy tank. It's about more than just feeling less stressed; it's about brightening your overall mood. Intentionally making room for these boosts is akin to keeping your internal "bank account" healthy, ensuring a richer life experience. This aligns with your brain's innate quest for balance. Faced with life's unpredictability, your brain instinctively seeks stability, adopting an "Okay, let's find our footing again" attitude. Engaging in activities you love, or that bring you peace, signals your brain to release dopamine and serotonin, the unsung heroes quietly working to alleviate stress and refuel your energy levels.

## Quick Hits to Get There

Boosting your energy isn't about wishful thinking; it's about committing with the same intensity as watching the finale of your favourite series. Here's how to make sure you get there:

- **Rally Your Squad.** Sharing your energy goals does more than just put words out there; it gears up your brain for action, making your ambitions solid and supported. It's like telling your brain, "We're in this", and having it prep for the journey.

- **Smartphone Smart You.** Use your phone smarter. Take a screenshot of Figure 2.1 and set it as your screensaver to keep the importance of energy management top of mind.
- **Be Water, My Friends.** Remember, the only constant in life is change. Water takes the shape of anything it enters. So, as your world spins and shifts, be ready to adjust your energy strategy too. New challenges? New opportunities? Time to recalibrate.

Think about Edison's famous advice on not throwing in the towel, paraphrased as: "I have not failed. I've just found 10,000 ways that won't work". This isn't just motivational fluff; it's solid brain training. Each time you double down, tweak your approach and give it another shot, your brain is hitting the gym. It's forging new pathways, getting tougher, and learning how to handle challenges better.

So, when you're committed to managing your energy smartly, you're doing more than just keeping your spirits up. You're essentially putting your brain through boot camp, making it sharper and more capable of tackling whatever comes its way.

## Case Study: The Everyday Superhero's Quest for Energy

I'd like to talk about my client Sarah. You might not personally know her, but she's the type you'd find familiar. She's the archetype of "keeping all the balls in the air", balancing reports and recipes with a resolve that's both awe-inspiring and slightly intimidating. Sarah's the hero in her own life, skilfully manoeuvring the corporate jungle and the wilds of parenthood with equal fervour.

However, like every superhero, Sarah faced her kryptonite: the unyielding demands of life that left her as drained as a smartphone at the end of a long day. Striving for professional success while ensuring she didn't miss a beat in her children's lives felt like an endless race.

We met after I gave a presentation at her company, which led her to seek my counsel. Standing on the brink of burnout, she faced it as if it were an unbeatable foe. It was clear she needed something more than just quick fixes. She needed a sustainable plan. That's when I introduced her to the Power Protect strategy. It wasn't polished or perfect back then, but the foundational idea immediately clicked with Sarah.

Captivated by visuals, Sarah loved the concept of seeing herself as a rechargeable battery. It's a simple analogy but think about it; batteries require management to stay charged. Managing energy isn't just about avoiding burnout; it's about ensuring you have enough power for the things that truly matter.

Sarah took small, meaningful steps to begin. Each morning, she started by checking in with herself, much like glancing at her phone's battery icon. This tiny ritual became her guiding star, helping her make choices that aligned with her energy levels throughout the day. Cutting down on the sheer volume of daily decisions she made was the first and easiest cull. She knew that every decision took a hit on her battery reserves, from what to put in the kids' packed lunch box, choosing what to wear, searching for keys, kids' shoes or homework, and each would silently zap her energy. So, she began to plan ahead by creating a meal plan and organising her work outfits on rotation and so on. In the office, she looked for ways to delegate more and get her team members to run decisions by each other first before coming to her to reduce her decision-making fatigue.

Soon Sarah began to recognise other culprits also quietly draining her energy. The endless cycle of social media scrolling, getting caught up in other people's dramas, and the negative influence of a pessimistic friend were subtly sapping her vitality. These seemingly minor activities culminated into major culprits behind her energy depletion, a reality she had remained oblivious to until we talked it through.

This newfound awareness brought Sarah to her first major turning point. The journey, of course, wasn't without its bumps. Challenges like perfectionism and a growing to-do list loomed large. And not every strategy was a win; some days, the crossword puzzles that usually recharged her felt like a chore, and long chats with a friend sometimes missed the mark.

Then there was the constant worry about her kids; like a persistent background noise that never fades. Will they make friends? Are they keeping up in school? This worry is the soundtrack of parenting, always playing on repeat. Sarah decided to turn down the volume by focusing on strengthening her communication with her kids, their teachers, and anyone who's part of their world. She reminded herself that parental concern was part of the job but also recognised the importance of allowing her children the space to grow and learn from their experiences.

She also acknowledged that managing her energy was crucial to keep up with her fast-paced life, a responsibility she alone can shoulder. But most importantly, Sarah became acutely aware that not every day was a carbon copy of the last, and her energy-replenishing strategies needed to adjust accordingly. It's like her energy needs had their own mood swings. Crossword puzzles and long chats with a friend were her go-to energy boosters, but even they weren't foolproof. She learned to ride the wave, adapting her strategies to match her current needs. Through the highs and lows, Sarah discovered that her most reliable source of energy came from within. By consciously choosing where to spend her energy, she found herself more equipped to face whatever life threw her way—with a smile that's genuine and a step that's light.

Sarah's story is a mirror reflecting our own struggles and triumphs in managing energy. It highlights that with a mix of smart planning, the willingness to pivot, and keen self-insight, conquering the chaos is within reach. More so, it brings home the powerful truth that despite our packed schedules, intentionally taking a moment to tune in to our inner needs and caring for them might just be the most protective thing we do—both for ourselves and those around us.

# 3 | Energy Playlist: Nail Your Day, Your Way

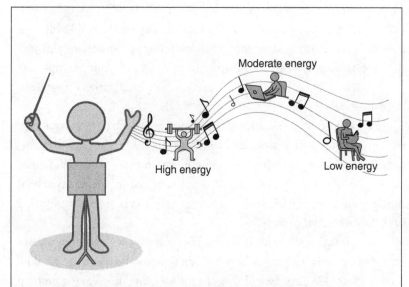

**Figure 3.1  The Energy Playlist**

**When to Use.**   For the times you need to power up, get back on track, and amp up your energy.

Have you ever come across the term *enantiodromia* before? Although it's often associated with psychology, its origins can be traced back to the insights of Greek philosophy.

> **Enantiodromia:** *the tendency of things to change into their opposites, especially as a supposed governing principle of natural cycles and of psychological development. (Oxford University Press, 2024)[1]*

This ancient idea remains surprisingly relevant today in understanding the complexities of life. It proposes that any force or circumstance, when pushed to its extreme, has a tendency to transform into its opposite; much like the effect of a pendulum swinging back and forth.

So, why should enantiodromia matter to you?

Consider your own energy levels for a moment. Many of you experience fluctuations in your vitality. One day you're riding high on the waves of boundless energy; ideas popping, productivity through the roof, feeling unstoppable. Then, out of nowhere, your get-up-and-go has left the building, and what was once effortless now feels insurmountable.

This continuous rise and fall, this constant oscillation, is your very own encounter with enantiodromia. As instinctive as the act of breathing, it resembles a pendulum swinging between two extremes. The key doesn't lie in resisting these inevitable swings but in adeptly synchronising your actions with your current energy levels, thus harmonising with this universal principle.

Now, imagine if you were to organise your day as if to curate a playlist for your different moods. You wouldn't choose heavy metal to wind down before sleep, nor would you opt for soothing tunes to get fired up for a workout, right? In a similar vein, it's wise to align, where possible of course, your tasks with how your energy levels fluctuate throughout the day. So, when you're full of energy, why not take advantage of that time to tackle ideas or challenging projects? Then, at times when your energy's low, focus on activities that don't require deep thinking.

The concept of creating an *Energy Playlist* clicked for me when I noticed my own energy levels were all over the place. It feels like

---

[1] Oxford University Press, 2024. *Definition of Enantiodromia*. Oxford University Press. https://www.oxfordreference.com/display/10.1093/oi/authority.20110803095750583.

flipping through Spotify, hunting for the perfect track which hits just the right spot for the mood I'm in. When you nail it, it's magic—the moment you and the music sync up perfectly.

When I tuned into my energy, I discovered that each day had its rhythm, with highs and lows creating my own special soundtrack. Embracing these fluctuations, instead of resisting them, brought about more of a sense of calm and stability into my routine.

This subtle change in viewpoint quickly evolved into a potent strategy within my toolkit for self-improvement. Sure, it's not ground-breaking, but matching activities with my natural energy patterns felt genuine and uniquely mine. It emphasises the importance of finding a rhythm that fits you perfectly; isn't that how the most effective self-improvement journeys should be?

## Syncing Your Day with the Energy Playlist

Think of your energy levels as a dynamic wave, rather than a steady stream—this insight from neuroscience isn't just food for thought; it helps shift the focus from just "getting things done" towards riding our energy wave with our natural rhythmic patterns.

Now, you might be wondering: "Interesting idea, but how does it actually fit into my life?" Enter the Energy Playlist strategy: a playful yet strategic way to align your daily tasks with your body's own cadence.

### *Tune into Your Day's Rhythm*

**High-Energy Tracks.**   These are your power hours when you're all in. Assigning tasks that demand your full attention and energy go here. Think of these moments like those pulse-pounding tracks that make you feel unstoppable. For some of you, inspiration may strike in the calm of morning, when the world's still asleep and your thoughts can take centre stage. For others, you may hit your stride in the exhilarating aftermath following a workout, carried by a surge of endorphins.

Night owls? Your prime time may arrive when others are winding down, revelling in the tranquillity of evening hours. But whenever it happens, these high-energy phases are meant for tackling the heavy lifts; like those complex assignments that demand focused attention and perhaps even spark some excitement.

**Moderate-Energy Tracks.** Then we hit a balance. Tasks here require focus but not your full mental horsepower. It's like the background music that keeps you in motion, ensuring progress without draining your reserves. This phase is ideal for routine tasks that keep the gears of your day greased and moving.

**Low-Energy Tracks.** And then there are times you need to take it easy and slow down. These are the moments when you can handle tasks that don't require mental effort, which is great when you start feeling tired. The key is to reduce the pace without stopping, so you can keep being productive while also saving your energy.

**Application.** When I hit my stride, it's full throttle. Writing in-depth articles, cooking up innovative ideas for future projects, or putting together killer speaker presentations. These activities hog all my brain power; they're my day's headliners, demanding the spotlight. To help jumpstart my brain into a focused mode, I pick a music playlist that I only use when I'm focusing. Much like Pavlov's dogs learned to react to a bell through conditioning, my brain immediately locks in. As the day transitions and my energy levels settle, it's a perfect backdrop for stuff like research and reading or catching up with my team. Yes, they need my focus, but they don't drain all my energy. They form consistent background music that keeps my day flowing smoothly.

As the day winds down, so does my energy, making it the perfect backdrop for those low-effort yet necessary tasks. This is when I sift through emails that require minimal cognitive lift, or lay the groundwork for the following day with some light planning. It's a time to lean into a slower pace, allowing both mind and body to ease into restfulness while preserving a reserve of energy for the evening ahead.

I recognise that not everyone will have the luxury to match their tasks with their natural energy cycles, particularly in rigid work environments. If that's you, fret not. Try to identify even small windows during your day when you do have some control. Perhaps it's addressing a challenging task right after your morning coffee, or saving easier tasks for that post-lunch slump. Even these modest adjustments can make a difference in how you feel and perform throughout the day.

**Insight.** It's essential to acknowledge that your brain has natural limitations in the amount of focus and energy it can sustain; experiencing with it highs and lows. By aligning your tasks to match these natural energy shifts, you're effectively leveraging the capabilities of your brain's rhythm. It's not about boosting productivity; it's about working smarter by understanding how your brain naturally operates, making sure you're not overexerting it during low phases and capitalising on those times when it's firing on all cylinders.

### Music and Mental Energy

Indeed, what would the Energy Playlist strategy be without the essential component—music? For those of you who find solace and inspiration in melodies, you're in luck, the intersection of neuroscience and music opens up a world of possibilities.

There have been many studies in the field of music therapy that have demonstrated that engaging with certain types of music can significantly reduce signs of stress, like lowering blood pressure, decreasing cortisol levels, and enhancing heart rate variability. These changes in the body pave the way for a reduction in anxiety and promote a sense of relaxation. Intuitively, this idea also resonates with me because, as author Hans Christian Anderson once wrote: "Where words fail, music speaks". And it often touches places that words alone cannot reach. *Weightless* is a song by Marconi Union, which is frequently mentioned as an example when talking about how music can have a calming influence. The precise data on its effectiveness is limited, due to a shortage of peer-reviewed studies available. However, there seems to be a general consensus amongst music therapists, sound therapists, researchers, and psychologists that carefully curated melodies such as this one can play a powerful role in combating stress.

Binaural beats are another noteworthy example of an auditory phenomenon. This is when two different frequencies are played in each ear, and the brain perceives a tone that represents the mathematical difference between the two. It is suggested that this can help induce feelings of relaxation, concentration, or vitality, depending on the beats' frequency. By listening to beats that match your desired energy level—opting for higher frequencies for high-energy tracks and lower ones for winding down—you can help guide your brain into an ideal state for the task at hand. This is particularly useful for entering a deep-work mode during your high-energy phases or gently winding down during low-energy periods.

But whatever your jam is, thoughtfully integrating music into your daily routine adds another tool to your arsenal, allowing you to surf the waves of your energy peaks and valleys more seamlessly.

## Case Study: Rhythms of a Busy Dad

I recall with striking clarity the day Alex first walked into my office. Collapsing in the chair across from me, he let out a deep sigh that seemed to echo the weight he was carrying. His eyes were filled with an urgent longing for a change, and his story resonated deeply; not just with me but with many stories I've encountered over the years.

Alex epitomised a determined professional, seeing his career flourish through unwavering ambition and hard work. At the same time, he balanced the responsibilities of being a father to three children, managing the demands of work, family life, and looking after his ageing parents. As he would so often tell me, his days were a blur of early-morning meetings, school drop-offs, late-night work commitments, and everything in between. The stress was palpable not only on him but also on his partner, who frequently bore the brunt of his absences. She would often use humour as a coping mechanism by joking with others and telling them she was a single mother, and that really saddened him.

Life was throwing challenge after challenge for Alex, and he was wrestling to stay afloat. During one of our sessions, we explored the Energy Playlist approach. He had once casually mentioned needing to update his gym playlist but lacked the time, which hinted at his interest in music. Alex instantly saw the appeal of this idea. Actually, it was like a eureka moment for him—aligning his day's tasks to match how energised he felt at different times. This wasn't just another technique; it felt as though it was designed with him in mind.

He started mapping out his mornings for tackling high-priority work tasks, client meetings and problem-solving, while his mind was freshest, then, during his midday break, he used the time for doctor's appointments or simply checking in with elderly parents, which needed a different kind of energy. As the afternoon energy dip hit, he focused on lighter work tasks that didn't demand as much mental strain. Two evenings a week were dedicated solely to his family; helping with homework, engaging in activities with his kids, and spending quality time with his wife.

At first, this approach struck the right chord. Mornings were a crescendo of productivity as Alex readily tackled high-energy jobs. However, the afternoons were frequently fraught with complications. Balancing work and family responsibilities while sticking to his Energy Playlist proved difficult. Unexpected circumstances, such as a child's illness or a parent's doctor visit, frequently disrupted his carefully planned schedule.

Not one to throw in the towel, Alex, rather ingeniously, formed a pact with colleagues facing similar struggles, creating what he affectionately called the "Energy Playlist crew". This group became a support system, swapping energy tips and providing encouragement through the inevitable days when things went awry. These exchanges evolved into a source of inspiration and motivation, aiding them in remaining committed to refining their Energy Playlists.

Alex learned something important from this experience; flexibility is the way to go. There really is no such thing as a perfect day. What truly matters at the end of the day is being able roll with the flow and adjust when necessary. Life's demands can change in an instant, so it's crucial to be able to update his Energy Playlist. Understanding that family obligations can sometimes come first, he became skilled at rearranging his schedule and priorities as needed, with the support of his friends, who helped him feel okay about it.

Alex's story isn't about mastering some kind of secret productivity hack. It's about embracing the unpredictability of life, and sometimes accepting that being a slightly offbeat dad and a deadline warrior is okay. The Energy Playlist strategy is less about strict scheduling and more about moving in sync with life's unforeseeable beats.

Today, Alex keeps at it, armed with his playlist and his crew, riding the ups and downs of work and family life. He's learned that it's not about avoiding the skips and scratches of a busy life but learning to move with them.

PART

II

# Supercharge Your Productivity

This section (Chapters 4–6) delves into the multifaceted aspects of productivity, presenting ideas to enhance how efficiently and effectively you work. You'll learn how to leverage patterns, emotions, and even procrastination to increase your productivity.

You will discover that productivity doesn't always require passion by recognising the significance of pattern recognition. This realisation can help empower you to spot and leverage recurring patterns in your day-to-day tasks and surroundings to achieve more desirable outcomes.

Emotional connection is also emphasised as a key factor for boosting productivity. Finding pleasure and meaning, even within those ordinary activities, can help uncover new ways to establish a more inspiring routine. You will learn practical strategies to transform your tasks into chances for development by aligning tasks with your motivators to maintain and sustain high productivity levels.

This section also explores our proclivity to postpone; uncovering both its detrimental and positive aspects. You will learn how to channel the energy that can arise from procrastination and turn it from a setback into a source of productivity.

Finally, you will be provided with practical tools to tackle feeling stuck and keep moving steadily, especially when time is running short. These tools aren't just superficial fixes; they offer real and proven techniques to help you move forward effectively, regardless of any constraints you might face.

Overall, this section will provide you with a comprehensive understanding of productivity, offering you the insights and skills to improve and optimise your daily workflow. You will be able to identify patterns, harness emotions, and tackle procrastination head-on, all while using practical tools to ensure consistent progress.

# 4 | No Passion, No Problem: The Power of Patterns

**Figure 4.1  The Power of Patterns Recognition**

**When to Use.**   You want to discover and cultivate your passions by leveraging your evolving interests and strengths.

Imagine, just for a moment, standing at a luxurious buffet spread, surrounded by colourful plates with a variety of flavours and textures from all around the world. Let's now suppose you're told you can only select one dish that must entirely satisfy you. This situation could feel a tad overwhelming, right? This is how many of us feel when we are attempting to pinpoint our actual passion—a quest that often leaves us feeling more confused than empowered.

However, what if the way we have gone about finding our passion has been misguided all along? What if it's not about anticipating that one big electrifying moment that changes our lives, but rather about a gradual day-by-day discovery of the many things we like, and what we're good at?

I came to realise that passion isn't simply handed to us all at once, perfectly formed and ready to go. Instead, it grows slowly as we go through life, sparked by our curiosity and influenced by the choices we make. This shift in outlook invites us to direct our attention away from chasing a preordained purpose, towards uncovering possibilities within ourselves.

Since our brains are incredibly versatile, capable of learning things and enhancing our existing knowledge. This hints at the idea that passion is a trait we can cultivate over time rather than something that just spontaneously arises.

My own journey, likely not too dissimilar to yours, has been anything but simple, lacking those "aha" moments. What I discovered instead is that passion, a genuine enduring kind, tends to develop like a friendship, deepening with experiences, interests, and unbridled curiosity. Letting my interests develop organically was truly what set me free.

## Mirror, Mirror: Explore Your Best Self

While supporting individuals in addiction recovery, emphasising their strengths has played a pivotal role in helping them regain self-confidence and find a new direction. It starts with recognising the potential within and nurturing it. Yes, easier said than done I quite agree. One effective method I've found to help do just that is the *Reflected Best Self Exercise.*[1] This activity involves seeking input from half a dozen people who know you well in different areas of your life, and whose opinion you trust, and asking them to share with you a time when they've seen you at your best and which strengths showed up.

If the idea of doing that is already giving you anxiety, you could be honest and tell them that while you feel really uncomfortable asking this, you realise this is an important step for your growth. The real magic happens once people start responding because you'll likely notice recurring themes in what they're saying. At this point remind yourself that they're telling you the truth, they are reflecting to you the goodness they see in you.

Let's face it: we often tend to be blind to our own brilliance, and if we let other people reflect on the strengths they admire in us through their eyes and call that out, well, it can open our eyes to qualities we never truly appreciated in ourselves. Remember, it's not about receiving praise (though, admittedly, that's always nice); it's about identifying recurring patterns of your skills and talents.

The inclusion of this exercise into group therapy sessions at the clinic had a profound impact on the people who once believed they had very little to contribute. Through highlighting each other's strengths, in a supportive setting, participants not only increased their self-confidence, but also built a close-knit community. This demonstrates that finding one's passion might just be about discovering the many ways we can shine in our own lives and in the eyes of others.

Years ago, when I first tried this reflective exercise, I found myself in quite the pickle—asking my close friends to point out my strengths felt downright bizarre. It's not every day you message your group chat, "Hey, what am I good at?" right? The awkwardness of it all was palpable, but I plucked up the courage and did it anyway. To my surprise, my friends spotted my talent for listening and untangling problems—qualities I somewhat recognised but never truly

---

[1] Quinn, R.E., Dutton, J.E., Spreitzer, G.M. et al. (2005). The Reflected Best Self Exercise™ (RBSE). Center for Positive Organizations, University of Michigan. Available at: https://reflectedbestselfexercise.com/.

gave myself credit for, until they were echoed back by those whose opinions I valued dearly. At first, their feedback felt exhilarating but as the days passed it became barely noticeable amongst the daily grind. However, these little nudges, over time, began to gently guide me away from the familiar world of finance—a place where I had grown uncomfortably comfortable—towards the unchartered territories of coaching and therapy. This unexpected shift had caught me off guard, bringing along its own set of uncertainties. Reflecting back on it now, I'm so thankful for that awkward ask! I never would have imagined that clumsy inquiry would, years later, lead to one of the most rewarding leaps of faith I've ever taken.

These days, whenever I share similar moments with my friends and clients of where I see them shine, it not only makes them happy and proud but also reinforces the value of recognising and encouraging our own strengths and those of others. Celebrating the abilities of those around us underlines the significance of providing encouragement and recognition.

So, if you're feeling unsure about what you're passionate about, try honing in on the things you're naturally good at. Find ways to weave these skills into your regular routine without stressing about how they align with your career trajectory. Pursue even the smallest of interests as they could unexpectedly merge into a passion that's truly your own.

Why not even consider giving the Reflected Best Self Exercise a shot? Seek feedback from those closest to you and remain open to where it might lead you. Learning about yourself in this way may uncover avenues of growth and development that have, until now, been obscured. Keep in mind also that it's completely natural for your interests to shift with time. As we journey through life our passions evolve, which only adds new depths to our lives.

## Case Study: Beyond the Lightning Bolt

Jose's story doesn't veer into the dramatic, yet it reflects a reality many of us face in the pace of modern life. She wasn't dealing with the darkest forms of substance abuse, but found herself in a cycle that's all too familiar: the end of each workday was marked by a few glasses of wine as her sole breather, her life segmented into anticipation of holidays, with each day melding indistinctly into the next without any real zest or distinction.

Her life was emblematic of the rat race—technically living but not quite alive, her career achievements a poor substitute for genuine fulfilment. The initial thrill of success had dulled over time, replaced by a nagging question: "Is this all there is?"

During our conversations it became clear that Jose needed more than a simple change of scenery; she needed a seismic shift in how she viewed things and lived her life. I felt trying out the Reflected Best Self Exercise would be a way to begin. Although she felt a bit shy and awkward at first, she understood the assignment and cautiously decided to ask people in her circle for their feedback on the moments when they saw her at her best.

The responses she got were really enlightening. Her co-workers appreciated her knack for easing conflicts at work, her friends admired her patience, tenacity, and the fact she could always find humour in just about anything. Her family highlighted her talent in photography and storytelling and while these were adolescent hobbies she hadn't thought about for quite a while, she now reflected on them with self-appreciation and nostalgia. While these talents may not have seemed exceptional, to Jose they were truly hers—since they brought joy to those around her, maybe they could also bring back some of that joy into her own life.

This fresh realisation began to motivate Jose to step out of her stagnant routine. Recognising that life offered more than the golden handcuffs of her job and her uninspiring evening rituals, she began incorporating her innate talents into her life both inside and outside of work. Over the months that followed, she joined a local photography club and started a humorous blog where she shared anecdotes that captured ordinary moments from her own perspective.

Now, I hate to rain on this parade, but alas, no, Jose didn't undergo a sudden overnight transformation, nor did this all lead to a fairytale ending where every day was filled with happiness and satisfaction. Instead, it unfolded slowly, with ups and downs along the way. However, during the peaks, she reconnected with unearthed aspects of herself that had been buried beneath the dull routine of her past life. Her days became more vibrant, enriched by moments of connection and creativity unrelated to her work or societal pressures. Jose's story is the recognition that fulfilment often lies in the smallest of details of our daily lives. She, of course, still looks forward to her holidays, but she no longer lives for them. Nowadays, she finds regular small escapes and reasons to be joyful in aligning her interests with her natural strengths, a testament to the power of reacquainting ourselves with the parts of us that the rat race often obscures.

# 5 | Pleasure-Driven Productivity: Let's Get Emotional

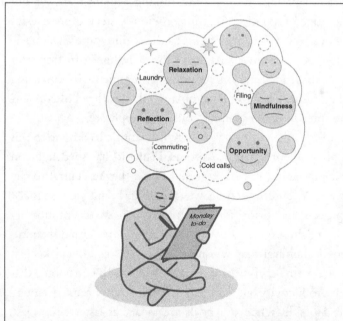

**Figure 5.1 Pleasure-Driven Productivity**

**When to Use.** You crave a productivity approach that mixes pleasure with getting stuff done.

There's this old-school belief plastered all over the productivity world: set goals, chase them down like your life depends on it, and boom, success is yours. Sound familiar? If you're like me, or countless others I've spoken with, you might just find this approach feels more like trying to get out of a maze with no exits than actually making strides towards success. I've been down the road of setting sky-high goals more times than I'd care to count, only to trip over my own feet at the first hurdle. It wasn't just disappointing, it was disorienting; it felt like I was perpetually running around in circles rather than crushing my goals. However, everything changed when I stopped fixating on what I wanted to accomplish and started thinking about how I wanted to feel each day. That's when I found an approach that truly connected with me.

Ditching the rigid checklist, I started to ask myself: How do I want to feel today? This wasn't about finding a perfect answer but exploring a range of emotions that unconsciously steered my day. It's like finding out your GPS has been set to the scenic route all along—and suddenly, you're not in such a hurry to reach the destination after all. This pivot from focusing on concrete achievements to nurturing my desired emotional states opened up a whole new level of connection that no spreadsheet or planner could ever replicate.

And in case you're curious, yes, there is scientific backbone to this emotional pivot. Neuroscientist Antonio Damasio has shed light on how our feelings aren't just background noise; they're central to the decisions we make and the actions we take.[1] Our brains are essentially wired to process and prioritise emotions. When we're emotionally invested in our daily experiences, our brain rewards us with dopamine, that feel-good chemical that whispers: "This feels right; let's keep it going". It's the brain's own way of nudging us towards behaviours that enhance our productivity but it does so through positive reinforcement.

On the flip side, when our goals are as dry as last week's toast, we're just putting our brain's logic centre to work. And while it's good at its job, it can get swamped, leading to that worn-out feeling where even choosing what to have for lunch feels like a big deal.

---

[1] Damasio, A. (1999). *The Feeling of What Happens: Body and Emotion in the Making of Consciousness*. Fort Worth, TX: Harcourt College Publishers.

In essence, if you treat your goal setting like it's a math problem, you might be left feeling disconnected. However, focusing on how you wish to feel each day can help connect your actions with your feelings. By adopting this perspective, setting goals shifts from a mechanical checklist into an exploration closely intertwined with your beliefs and emotions. This shift fuels a motivation that's not only stronger but also more enduring.

Perhaps it's time to step away from the outdated "do this and achieve that" mindset and discover your own style, something that stirs up excitement and moves you forward. Personally, I have found it beneficial to focus on the emotions I want to experience each day. Now, for you, it might be something completely different. Maybe try setting a daily "theme" based on what you want to accomplish that day; for example, "creativity" for a brainstorming session, or "connection" for a day of interactions. The trick is to allow your feelings to lead the way for a productivity rhythm that's uniquely yours. This approach can help turn even the most hectic days into opportunities for meaningful engagement and progress.

Now, you may be thinking this is all well and good but how can I realistically make this lofty idea work, especially with a mile-long to-do list staring me down? I appreciate it might seem like a leap from theory to daily practice but don't sweat it, I've got you covered.

## Getting Things Done: A Fresh Look at Routine

How can you spice up your habits to freshen up your approach to productivity? Well, those repetitive and mundane tasks you often do without thought, the ones that seem never-ending and uninspiring, actually hold the potential for change. It's not about pushing yourself harder, it's about seeing your routines through a brand-new lens. This stands to reason, since throughout human history, the greatest of achievements have been accomplished on the back of steadfast routines. Just consider the masterpiece painting of the Sistine Chapel ceiling, which took Michelangelo four intense years to complete. His unwavering commitment and daily dedication resulted in one of the most celebrated masterpieces in art history.

I appreciate that what I am about to say next may be terribly unexciting, but it is within the very humdrum routine of your everyday life that you'll find fertile ground for growth if you choose to see it that way. Your day-to-day life is where character is shaped, endurance is nurtured, and the groundwork for triumph is laid. Finding pleasure in the ordinary isn't just about being patient, but about making a deliberate decision to see the value in every moment. Indeed, it is within these quiet, often overlooked, endeavours that you define yourself and establish your presence in the world.

If you want to transform your tasks into chances for development, here are five ways to add meaning and feeling to even the most mundane activities.

### *Tap into the "Anticipation Effect"*

You can significantly enhance your dopamine levels by leveraging the power of the "anticipation effect", a fascinating little-known neuroscience hack. You see, your brain doesn't just release dopamine when you experience joy but also in anticipation of it. For instance, have you ever noticed that when you are feeling excited it is really hard to sleep? Well, that's dopamine doing its rounds.

This little piece of wisdom has really changed how I start my mornings. Nowadays I kick off each day with an eager question: "What new opportunities await me today?" It's not about staying positive; it's my conscious effort to bring excitement into the options of my day. By adopting this mindset, you can steer clear of falling into the pattern of thinking that usually limits your vision of what's achievable, and instead it allows you to uncover your potential. This subtle change not only sparks your imagination, by prompting you to spot possibilities in unexpected places, but also ignites your drive. Turning mundane routines into avenues for growth.

For my clients, who often find themselves mired in monotony, but hesitant to shake things up, I frequently suggest making a "Surprise Me" list. It's an easy practice that involves noting down small, manageable experiments they can introduce into their lives, like checking out a new place for lunch, taking a different route home, or listening to an unfamiliar musician or podcast. These minor tweaks have the power to bring unexpected delight into their days, by igniting a sense of wonder that breathes freshness into their routines. Indeed, it is these quiet wins that set the stage for the big wins.

By looking at things from this point of view, you can greatly enrich your life. Because, being open to novel experiences and nurturing your curiosity, it does more than just engage your mind; it helps you create neural connections, which keeps your mind sharp. Furthermore, it creates opportunities for new possibilities and broadens your perception of what you can achieve.

### Elevate the Ordinary

This idea takes you even deeper because it suggests that true fulfilment lies in infusing joy into every task, no matter how routine or trivial it might appear. Can you imagine reframing the pursuit of happiness into finding happiness in the pursuit itself? Rather than waiting for those big, joyous occasions to come your way, what if you could uncover pleasure in everyday experiences, no matter how simple they appear to be?

Take, for example, Marie Kondo, the Japanese organising consultant and author. In her book *The Life-Changing Magic of Tidying Up: The Japanese Art of Decluttering and Organizing* (Ten Speed Press, 2011),[2] she transformed the task of cleaning into a life-altering belief. Through her *KonMari* technique, she motivates individuals to hold onto those things that bring them happiness. This method shifts the chore of tidying and simplifying into a voyage of self-discovery and attentive living. She has demonstrated to millions of people around the globe that something as basic as sifting through old clothes can evolve into an opportunity for emotional release and personal growth.

Let's suppose you treat every email you write as not just another thing to get through but an opportunity to improve your communication skills. Every spreadsheet a puzzle that can help sharpen your analytical thinking. And even those dishes you are washing? What if they could serve as a quiet moment of mindfulness, finding contentment in the clean and simple?

Before starting your next task, take a second to spot something good about it. Maybe it's a chance to improve a skill or a way you're making someone's day a little easier, or it simply gives you a quiet moment of focus.

---

[2] Kondo, Marie. The Life-Changing Magic of Tidying Up: *The Japanese Art of Decluttering and Organizing*. Berkeley: Ten Speed Press, 2011.

I realise this perspective may appear super idealistic. I assure you it's backed by scientific research, such as that published in the *Journal of Happiness Studies*, showing that individuals who find meaning and joy in their daily lives are genuinely happier.[3] Therefore, it's more than just a nice thought, it's a validated approach to improving your overall happiness and well-being.

Embracing this outlook on your daily habits and routines leads to a change in mindset. Because you move away from perceiving them simply as tedious activities, towards recognising them as opportunities for self-improvement, learning, and joy. This mindset requires you to turn every chore into an adventure, safe in the knowledge of knowing that your brain instinctively responds positively to finding meaning and pleasure in the little things.

Coming from a finance career, I really get how hard it can be to take all this on board. The challenge of seeing everyday tasks as opportunities for celebration becomes even harder when you are dealing with tight deadlines, back-to-back meetings, or managing personal commitments. This difficulty is a genuine reflection of the complex balancing act demanded by modern living.

Yet, the goal here isn't to achieve an overnight transformation but to slowly integrate small changes in how you approach and engage with your daily activities. It could start with something as practical as pausing for a deep breath before tackling a pile of emails, or taking a moment to recognise the effort and creativity that goes into every project.

Yes, it can be challenging to maintain this mindset all the time, especially when you're swamped with tasks. But there's a real benefit in trying to bring this way of thinking into your lives bit by bit. By treating every email, every task, and every chore as a little victory, a sign that you're alive and kicking, you start living by a philosophy that mixes brain science with the timeless search for what life's all about. This way, even the boring stuff feels important, like it's a key

---

[3] Krasko, J., Intelisano, S. and Luhmann, M. (2022). When happiness is both joy and purpose: The complexity of the pursuit of happiness and well-being is related to actual well-being. *Journal of Happiness Studies* 23(6): 3233–3261. https://doi.org/10.1007/s10902-022-00541-2.

chapter in your life story, giving your everyday tasks more meaning and purpose.

### Single-Tasking in a Multi-Tasking World

Whenever we talk about being productive, our minds can often jump to multi-tasking. However, the true secret to productivity is not in juggling tasks, which is, quite frankly, exhausting, but in our ability to fully concentrate on one task at a time. It's all about giving our attention to each activity, which ultimately improves the quality of our work and overall life experience.

Support for this perspective comes from research published in the *Journal of Experimental Psychology*. The research highlights that individuals who focus on one task excel over those who try to multi-task.[4] The reasoning behind this is quite simple. Multi-tasking puts a strain on your abilities, resulting in lapses of attention and memory that impede your effectiveness. In today's age, filled with distractions, this knowledge serves as a reminder of the drawbacks of splitting your focus.

So, before you pride yourself on your multi-tasking prowess, it's worth considering that less might indeed be more, and adopting a single-tasking approach may actually be the more productive choice in your hectic life.

But single-tasking is not just about doing; it's about being—fully present and immersed in the task before you. Think about an athlete in the heat of competition, there's a reason they often describe feeling "in the zone"—a state of absolute focus where distractions cease to exist and performance peaks. This level of presence taps into a deep well of energy, driving you towards your objectives without the cost of exhaustion.

The advantages of this laser-focused approach also extend beyond boosting productivity. Contrast having a conversation peppered with smartphone glances, to one where each party is fully engaged, hanging onto every word. The latter doesn't just exchange information; it's creating an atmosphere of genuine engagement and mutual

---

[4] Rogers, R.D. and Monsell, S. (1995). Costs of a predictable switch between simple cognitive tasks. *Journal of Experimental Psychology: General* 124(2): 207–231. doi: 10.1037/0096-3445.124.2.207.

respect. This isn't abstract philosophy; it's the very essence of human connection.

So, when the urge to juggle tasks comes up, pause for a moment to reflect on these benefits and immerse back once more into what you were doing. It's quite easy to forget sometimes that life isn't just a series of tasks to be completed but a collection of moments to be genuinely lived.

### Fear to Fuel

Here you stand on the brink of stepping into the spotlight, and all of a sudden the fear of underperforming creeps in and tightens its grip around you. This chokehold isn't only frustrating, it's downright paralysing. It's as if your own mind is blocking you from tapping into your true capabilities. What if I told you the key to unshackling yourself from this mental incarceration doesn't solely rely on a collection of motivational platitudes, but has its foundations deeply rooted in positive psychology?

Now, I hate being told to be positive as much as the next person. Suffice to say I needed a bit more convincing of the psychological effects of cultivating a positive mindset, over and above feeling good. Well, I didn't have to look too far, an intriguing study from the University of North Carolina reveals that it transforms the very architecture of our brain.[5] When you open your mind to looking for the good, you become aware of possibilities and answers that were previously obscured. Your creativity blossoms and your ability to solve problems becomes more accurate. It can feel like a light has been switched on by revealing paths that were once hidden in plain sight.

Now, think about the dialogue you have with yourself in those critical pre-performance moments of anticipation, like a job interview, presentation, or meeting. Ever caught yourself muttering, "I hope I don't mess this up", right before facing a big moment? What if you turned that narrative on its head asserting, "I've got this and am ready to do my absolute best". Seems overly simplistic, right? Yet, the ripple effect of this small change is anything but.

---

[5] Fredrickson, B.L. and Losada, M.F. (2005). Positive affect and the complex dynamics of human flourishing. *American Psychologist* 60(7): 678–686. doi: 10.1037/0003-066X.60.7.678. Erratum: *American Psychologist* (2013) 68(9): 822. PMID: 16221001; PMCID: PMC3126111.

This act of relabelling your fear as excitement is you essentially performing a psychological sleight of hand. Your body doesn't know how to distinguish between fear and excitement because both emotions trigger similar physiological responses, such as a racing heart rate, a rush of adrenaline and heightened alertness. The only key difference is how you interpret these signals. By coaxing your brain to shift its gaze from looming threats to sparkling opportunities—a minor, yet powerful, adjustment that can substantially influence what happens next.

This theory, as we explored in Chapter 2, is reinforced by research conducted at Harvard Business School, which validates the effectiveness of this "anxiety reappraisal", revealing that a bit of strategic self-talk can dramatically boost your performance.[6] It's not just a mind trick; it's a proven strategy to dial up your performance.

So, when you feel those butterflies in your stomach, remember: you have the power to change how you think. Instead of seeing fear, try to see the excitement of an opportunity. This is a scientifically supported tactic for unlocking the latent potential of your brain and boosting your productivity like never before.

### The Two-Minute Mental Replay

Here's a strategy so effortless that it doesn't ask you to find extra time but smartly capitalises on the snippets of time you already have at your disposal. It's called the *Two-Minute Mental Replay*, attributed to Shawn Achor, a well-known speaker in the field of positive psychology and author of *The Happiness Advantage* (Crown Currency, 2010),[7] and it's as straightforward as it sounds.

We all encounter those pockets of time daily—moments when our bodies are on autopilot but our minds are up for grabs. Maybe it's the couple of minutes you spend staring at your coffee machine as it sputters awake, or those precious moments under the shower when the world outside doesn't exist. These bits of time, often dismissed as mundane, hold untapped potential for reflection.

---

[6] Brooks, A.W. (2014). Get excited: Reappraising pre-performance anxiety as excitement. *Journal of Experimental Psychology: General* 143(3): 1144–1158.
[7] Achor, S. (2010). *The Happiness Advantage: The Seven Principles of Positive Psychology That Fuel Success and Performance at Work*. Crown Currency.

Select one of these moments—just one to start with. Rather than letting your thoughts run wild or reaching for your phone, dedicate two minutes to replay a snippet from your day. It could be zooming in on a meeting, a chat you had, or something you ticked off your list. Two-Minute Mental Replay is not to nit-pick or self-flagellate but to acknowledge. Spot a moment that made you feel competent or per-haps surprisingly satisfied.

This isn't an exercise in self-critique or adding more things to do. It's a gentle reminder for your brain to pause and pat itself on the back, almost on autopilot. I find myself using these slivers of time not just to reflect on my day's doings but on who I am being. It's all too easy to get caught in the cycle of doing, losing sight of the fact that our actions are but reflections of our inner selves. By pausing to reflect, we engage in a dialogue with ourselves that has the power to transform ordinary experiences, echoing the Zen teaching that profound truths are often found in the present moment and lie hidden in plain sight.

The beauty of the Two-Minute Mental Replay technique lies in its simplicity and adaptability. It effortlessly fits into the moments of your day, requiring just a gentle change in perspective. With practice, this method can subtly boost your mindfulness. Gratitude for your accomplishments also fosters a more efficient and optimistic outlook, without the need to carve out extra time in your calendar.

## Supercharging Your Productivity: The Pleasure-Driven Way

You've heard it a million times—discipline is key but they never want to tell you why. Discipline is basically you playing the long game. It's choosing to pass on what you want right now because you're eyeing something way better down the line. It's proof you're all in on your dreams, even on those days when you'd rather do anything but. Think of the "future you" as a building under construction, and every prom-ise the "current you" keeps is a brick in that building. That's where accountability emerges as an indispensable ally.

But accountability doesn't have to be that bitter medicine everyone makes it out to be. So, how do you turn it from a buzzkill into a booster? Here are three moves:

1. **Set Goals That Stir Your Soul.** We've all been there, setting goals because we think we should. But when your goals are wired to what really lights you up inside, they stick. They become more than just items on a to-do list; they're personal, they matter. And that connection? It's rocket fuel for keeping you honest with yourself.

2. **Spin Habits into Gold.** The backbone of getting things done? Rock-solid habits. And no, they don't have to feel like homework. Discover habits that not only propel you towards your goals but also feel good. Maybe it's taking a quick break to shake your body, releasing any build-up of tension and stress, decompressing between meetings, or regularly crediting yourself for the little wins, these habits should lift you up not weigh you down.

3. **Get By with a Little Help from Your Friends.** Sharing your goals with someone else adds a layer of "I got to do this" that's hard to ignore. It could be a buddy, a mentor, or even a group—just make sure it's someone who gets it. This kind of backup turns accountability into a shared journey, not a solo slog.

In the end, accountability in the work world (and beyond) is about creating a vibe where everyone wants to show up, not out of obligation but out of authentic desire. It's about transforming productivity from a badge of honour into a source of genuine satisfaction. And that shift? That's what pleasure-driven productivity is all about.

# 6

# From Paralysis to Progress: Tools for the Time-Pressed

**Figure 6.1   Paralysis to Progress**

**When to Use.**   Whenever you find yourself stuck or feeling overwhelmed and need to shift from inaction to making strides.

Let's face it, procrastination is a sneaky little comfort-zone conspirator, often masking our reluctance to face the discomfort associated with a task, such as fear of failure, rather than a genuine dislike for the task itself. It's kind of like a psychological game of hide-and-seek within our minds, where delaying offers a temporary refuge from having to deal with these uncomfortable emotions. Perhaps we convince ourselves we'll be better prepared, or in a better frame of mind, later on. A strategy that we all know typically backfires, as those difficult feelings only seem to intensify as the deadlines loom closer. Yet time and again we find ourselves falling into its trap.

When we take a look at the range of these difficult emotions that drive procrastination, they are both vast and varied. They can span from the dread of not succeeding, to overwhelm, boredom, and resentment, right the way up to the pull of remorse, where each of these sentiments plays a role in the act of procrastination.

However, just being aware of our proclivity to postpone is only the first step. The true challenge lies in transforming stagnation into action. This chapter examines effective strategies to confront procrastination directly.

But first, to procrastinate or not to procrastinate—isn't that the quintessential question that often troubles many of us? Although procrastination is typically seen as a productivity killer, could it also possibly be a sparker of creativity in disguise? Let's explore this a bit further.

## Procrastination Paradox: The Good, The Bad, and The Creative

I've repeatedly found myself on this dramatic seesaw, experiencing the highs of a last-minute stroke of brilliance—**The Good**—only to then crash into the sobering realisation that what I've produced under pressure could have been so much more. Therein lies **The Bad**—that oh so tricky balance of using procrastination as a creative springboard without falling victim to its seductive time-wasting allure.

Now, at this point, I think it's also worth considering the age-old ancient concept of *Wu Wei*, which is a principle rooted in Eastern philosophy that promotes the notion of "non-action" or "effortless action". This is far from promoting laziness, Wu Wei instead encourages us to take strategic pauses so that we can allow events to evolve and unfold more organically. This rather unconventional perspective, in contrast to our society's emphasis on busyness, embodies wisdom in deliberate inaction—**The Creative** force behind procrastination.

Certainly, numerous research studies back up the idea that allowing yourself time to think can truly kindle creativity. Allowing your thoughts the freedom to ruminate over certain problems helps your mind meander into new territories, potentially leading to insights that a harried pace would probably overlook. Like letting a fine wine breathe, some ideas simply require room to develop their full bouquet.

Now before you run ahead of yourself and decide to delay all your tasks in the name of creativity, don't forget that procrastination also has its bad side too. When you constantly put off tasks, you're left with those horrid negative feelings like guilt or stress for those missed opportunities. It's sort of like indulging in dessert before dinner; it feels really good in the moment but likely regretful later on.

So, the real question you have to ask yourself is this: "What's my position when armed with both my goal and my deadline?" If you're intentionally putting things off as a move to maybe gather further information or for preparation, you're on the right track. You are practising the art of waiting wisely—**The Good** in its purest form. If you're dodging the task because you'd rather watch paint dry than face it, well, let's just say it might be time to reassess your strategy.

If it makes you feel any better, even ancient thinkers like Aristotle wrestled with this human quirk, terming it *akrasia*, or acting against one's better judgement. This struggle between knowing what to do and doing it also aligns with contemporary neuroscience. It suggests our battle with procrastination isn't about laziness but how we manage inner conflict; a storyline that interweaves **The Bad** with **The Creative**.

Therefore, the next time you find yourself caught up in procrastination, ask yourself this: "Am I letting my mind wander freely or am I trying to avoid the challenge ahead?" Putting off tasks isn't necessarily a sign of being disorganised. Sometimes it can serve as a strategy that if used smartly, may ignite creativity and insight, as presented in Part III.

## Proven Strategies to Transform Procrastination into Action

I get it—you're always on the go, from the minute you wake up to when your day ends. There's just no time for long-winded self-help advice or complex routines. What you need are clear, hands-on strategies that fit into your fast-paced life without a fuss. And that's exactly what I've put together here. These aren't a random set of tips; they're a carefully curated set of tools, each sharpened by scientific research and polished by expert insights. They're not just superficial fixes; they're real and proven techniques designed to tackle procrastination head-on.

Do they require effort? Absolutely. Will they demand your commitment? Undeniably. But think about it—what's more motivating than the thought of finally gaining control of your time and productivity?

How about we kickstart this process with something really simple? An "initiation ritual" to get your day rolling right. This ritual could be anything that signals to your brain okay, it's go-time. For example, pour yourself a hot drink or open your calendar to today's date. This simple act strips away all the fuss and it clearly signals the shift from relaxation to productivity. It's your cue that says: "I'm now set to take on the day".

With this basic, but powerful, step, you're prepped and primed to dive into the tools I've selected for someone as driven and busy as you.

### *Leverage Cliffhanger Psychology*

Let's start by addressing the proverbial elephant in the room—the task that needs your attention. You can confront it directly with an approach that may seem unconventional but is proven to be highly successful. The key is not to pressure yourself into action; instead, it's about reassuring your mind that any discomfort is temporary, so promise yourself to dedicate only five minutes to it. Not to complete it all at once, just to start the process.

This approach isn't about deceiving yourself into working; it involves tapping into a phenomenon called the *Zeigarnik* effect.

> *The* Zeigarnik *effect, from Gestalt psychology, refers to the phenomenon where we tend to remember uncompleted or interrupted tasks better than completed tasks, often leading to a desire to resume them later.*[1]

Let me elaborate. Have you ever questioned why it's so hard to resist watching the next episode of your favourite TV series after a cliffhanger ending? Well, that's the Zeigarnik effect at play. Our minds are wired to seek closure; to see things through to the end. By dedicating just five minutes to a task you're satisfying this urge. Initiating something often triggers your brain's itch to want to finish it.

More often than not, what begins as a five-minute commitment can naturally extend into longer periods of engagement, effectively bypassing procrastination. This isn't about pressuring yourself into an hours-long marathon; it's about making the start of any task much less daunting. It taps into our love for those suspenseful cliffhangers by leveraging our brain's inherent need for resolution, essentially harnessing cliffhanger psychology in our favour.

But what if five minutes feels too much? Then why not scale it back to two minutes? This idea, conceived by David Allen, acclaimed author of *Getting Things Done*, postulates a straightforward principle: if it takes less than two minutes to complete a task, then do it immediately.[2] I find its brilliance lies not just in its simplicity but in its ability to build momentum. Often the starting of something is the most challenging part, however, once you're past that hurdle, keeping the ball rolling becomes much easier.

Even if you stop after two minutes, you have still made progress. Those two minutes might not seem like much in isolation, but replicate them over time, and they coalesce into substantial progress. The two-minute rule encourages a culture of action, breaking down the barriers of procrastination and inertia one step at a time, offering a

---

[1] Zeigarnik, B. (1927). Über das Behalten von erledigten und unerledigten Handlungen. *Psychologische Forschung* 9(1): 1–85.
[2] Allen, D. (2001). *Getting Things Done: The Art of Stress-Free Productivity*. New York: Penguin Books.

small win that plays into the same cliffhanger psychology but by providing immediate closure to those shorter tasks.

Every time you decide to begin, even if it's just for a short while, you find yourself in the midst of a story that your mind is driven to complete. Whether it results in tidying up a room or just getting started on it, writing a report or drafting the introduction, the key lies in leveraging your love for storylines to your advantage.

Whether you call it the 30-minute rule, the 5-minute rule, or the 2-minute rule, the core idea remains the same; we are enticing our minds into action with the promise of a brief commitment, directly tapping into cliffhanger psychology to make getting started less of a challenge and more of an intrigue.

### *Turn Feedback into Fuel*

The worry and anticipation of how our efforts will be received is often what stops us in our tracks. Can you imagine standing on a stage, seconds away from the curtain rising, not knowing whether you're about to face applause or a deafening silence? It's a familiar spot for many of us, from those who speak in front of crowds to anyone who's thrown their ideas into the ring at work. That moment before feedback hits is tense, filled with apprehension, and honestly, it doesn't get much easier with experience. Knowing that your work is about to be judged can be intimidating, regardless of how many times you've been there before.

Looking into some brain science sheds light on why we react so strongly to feedback. Our brains are wired for response and adaptation; it's part of our learning process. When we receive positive feedback, our brain makes us want to repeat what earned us that praise. Negative feedback, on the other hand, is like our brain hitting a big red panic button, preparing us to either defend ourselves or shut down. This instinctual reaction might have been useful way back when avoiding danger was a daily concern, but less so in today's world, especially in navigating office politics or public scrutiny.

Recognising this truth marks the first step in reshaping our perception of it. When we can fully grasp that our gut response to constructive criticism, or, as I prefer to call it, *insight through hindsight*, is part of our old survival mechanism, we allow ourselves to reframe feedback in a new light—as something that's meant to help us grow rather than bring us down. By choosing to perceive feedback as beneficial, we are essentially upgrading the operating system of our minds. This doesn't just change how we feel about feedback; it changes how we use it. We don't need to live in fear of it because we can learn to see it as an invaluable tool, a means to refine and improve our work and ourselves.

Bringing this into my therapeutic practice, I've seen first-hand the transformation that happens when we shift our view of feedback; it's like rediscovering yourself and finding ways to improve rather than stewing in doubt. It's somewhat parallel to the ancient quest of "know thyself", guiding us towards growth rather than wallowing in self-doubt. Suddenly, feedback doesn't seem so intimidating anymore; it becomes a lighthouse guiding you towards personal evolution.

This is all well and good, but as you and I both know, shifting that automatic knee-jerk response to feedback is anything but easy. It forces you to acknowledge that you're still figuring things out. You're facing a decision. Remain forever stuck in fear of receiving feedback, leading to a stagnant existence, or courageously brave the tremors of the uncertainties that lay ahead.

But how can you make feedback work for you, practically speaking? Let's take a look:

- **Start the Conversation Early.** Don't wait until your project is finished to ask for feedback. Kickstart conversations with your colleagues, or mentors, right from the get-go. Think of it as gathering their perspectives to enhance the quality of your work versus just seeking their approval.
- **Change the Lens.** Be proactive about changing how you view feedback. Stick reminders where you'll see them daily—yes, like those post-it notes on your monitor. The goal here is to condition your brain to welcome feedback as constructive coaching, not personal jabs. It's about setting up a mental environment where feedback is seen as a ladder rather than a critique of character. Even if the feedback isn't constructive or helpful, recognise that others are entitled to their perspectives. Your only focus should be on how you will use this information (if at all) to move you closer to where you want to be.

- **Act on It.** After you've collected those observations, it's time to get down to work and apply them practically. Divide your task into manageable parts using the advice as your roadmap. This not only helps you understand where you're headed but also makes diving into action seem like a simple move rather than a massive jump.

Making these slight adjustments can make a world of difference. By moving your attention away from the pressure of getting it right, towards continually enhancing your skillset, you begin to think less and less about what isn't working. Feedback then becomes a motivator for progress rather than a source of delay.

Think about this when you're caught in those brief lulls between meetings and looming deadlines. What if, instead of shying away from what makes you uncomfortable, you leaned into it? I'm proposing you do more than just tolerate feedback; I'm talking about actively chasing it down and using it as the powerful tool for growth that it really is. It's about having the guts to show the world the parts of yourself that are still under construction, to mess up occasionally because those mistakes—they're actually paving the way to you becoming better and doesn't that matter far more than any momentary awkwardness you may feel?

But if you still find yourself paralysed by a task, remember to reach out to someone whose perspective you value. Let their insights guide you, not as a spotlight on your insecurities, but think of it more as helpful direction when you're unsure which way to go.

### Plan for Failure

We all procrastinate from time to time, and a lot of that comes down to being scared of failing. It's a universal feeling. Since it is so common, here's a straightforward idea: Why not plan for failure?

Think about it. By introducing something like a "failure fund", you're not simply allowing yourself to fail, but rather you're making a tactical decision that accepts that not every shot you fire will be a hit. It's like saying, "Okay, I know some of these things might not pan out, but that's part of the process".

This strategy doesn't aim to cover up your failures or turn them into motivational slogans. It's really about seeing failure as a part of learning and moving forward. Imagine setting aside time or resources for projects that might not succeed. This is not because you want them to fail but because you know that even if things don't go as planned, there is wisdom and learning to be gained from things not going according to plan.

I understand this may seem a bit paradoxical. We're usually told to steer clear of failure at any cost, yet we are contemplating its inclusion in our approach. The thing is, we've come to understand the bigger picture, which is that each setback actually propels us closer to our goals, not away from them.

Why don't you consider putting some of your energy into ventures where the chance of failure is not just probable but expected? It's a calculated decision, like an investor spreading out their investments because they understand that not all of them will yield returns. However, it's within these setbacks that the greatest chances for development are hidden.

Isn't there a delicious irony in that? Society has a deeply ingrained belief that failure is a negative thing. Yet here I am actually promoting the idea of embracing it strategically. Think about the wisdom in this mindset. You're not just accepting failure; you're actively pursuing it knowing that each stumble gets you nearer to your end goals.

Looking at failure through the lens of neuroscience, embracing it triggers learning processes in your brain. When you examine your failures, you stimulate the area of your brain responsible for making decisions and solving problems, known as the prefrontal cortex. This not only enhances your flexibility but also builds up your ability to bounce back from challenges. It motivates you to confront failure head-on and say: "You don't determine my worth. I will turn you into a stepping stone towards achieving my goals".

Even the philosophical Stoics practised something known as *premeditatio malorum*, or the premeditation of evils, which involved reflecting on hardships. This wasn't meant for them to dwell on negativity but to lessen its effect and prepare them to respond constructively.

Likewise, having a "failure fund" helps you mentally and emotionally handle setbacks so that you can bounce back stronger instead of letting them hinder your progress.

Thinking about failure in this way isn't only to comfort yourself. It's also about preparing for the next significant breakthrough. It encourages you to take risks, try things, and acknowledge that progress often comes with obstacles along the way.

So, what if your next failure isn't the end of the road but a detour towards something even greater? The chance to learn something new, refine your approach, or uncover a solution you hadn't considered before is invaluable.

I encourage you to see beyond the immediate setback of failure. Look at it as vital fuel towards achieving something bigger and better. After all, the lessons learned from what didn't work out are often what lead you to your greatest successes. Can you afford to ignore the potential insights from your next misstep? I trust your answer is a resounding no.

### *Employ the "Failure to Action" Technique*

So, you're all set with your planned setbacks thanks to your "failure fund". It's now time to turn those obstacles into opportunities for growth. Let's zero in on that one task you've been avoiding, perhaps due to the fear of it not being good enough. Here's a suggestion: take a moment to imagine messing up that task. Seriously, visualise it. How does failure appear to you? Can you feel that sinking feeling in your stomach?

You might feel a rush of nervous energy, possibly mixed with a hint of unease. It's not exactly a pleasant sensation, but it sure does pack a punch. You could liken it to a morning wake-up call. No one really relishes being awakened by the sound of ringing in their ears. However, this alarm means that it's time to get moving and kick things into gear.

Here's where you shift your mindset from dreading failure to leveraging it as a catalyst for progress. Whenever you sense that familiar flutter of nervousness, see it as a poke. It's the moment to tackle that upcoming task head-on.

Here's how to put the *Failure to Action* strategy into practice:

- **Acknowledge the Alarm.** Recognise the anxiety for what it is—a signal to start. You might tell yourself, "Okay, this is my cue", and stand ready to tackle the task ahead.
- **Set Small Targets.** Break the big scary task into bite-sized pieces. If you need to write a presentation, start by outlining the main points off the top of your head. The idea is to take one small step as soon as you feel that "alarm".
- **Pair Action with a Reward.** Follow up your action with something nice, just like stretching after turning off your alarm. Have you written those key points? Treat yourself to a brief relaxation pause in a cosy corner or a hydration break—you've responded to the "alarm".
- **Rinse and Repeat.** Then expect another obstacle. Harness the momentum from conquering the last difficulty to tackle this fresh challenge. Repeat this cycle; action, reward, next action, and continue moving through these stages until you finish.

By applying the Failure to Action method, you're not just sitting around and hoping for motivation to magically appear. Instead, you're turning your doubts into a fuel that *propels* you towards getting things done. This strategy isn't limited to tackling those tasks that you would rather avoid; it also chips away at the fear of failure itself by showing you that progress is possible regardless of the challenges that await you.

This is more than just another hack. You are fundamentally changing how you deal with and conquer the challenges that life throws your way.

### The "Action Anchoring Technique"

And finally, I've talked a lot about dealing with failure and overcoming it. Let's wrap it up nicely with the *Action Anchoring Technique*. It's an approach that helps you avoid magnifying problems in your mind by getting out of your head and into your body.

Your brain loves blowing things out of proportion, especially when it involves tasks you'd rather avoid. By shifting your focus to physical activities, you bypass all the mental theatrics. It's not about deceiving yourself; it's about aligning with your instinctive human drive to move and do stuff.

Here's the breakdown:

- **Kick Off with Something Physical.** Start with an action that's so simple it feels almost too easy. If you're dreading starting an email, just placing your hands on the keyboard is a good first step. Or if you're avoiding that run, getting your trainers on and standing outside is the move. This action is your anchor—it's real, it's tangible, and it's a reminder that every big thing starts small.
- **Ride the Momentum.** Once you've taken that first step, keep going with whatever comes next, no matter how small. The idea is that starting creates momentum, making it easier to continue. If you've started typing, keep at it even if it's just rambling at first. If you're standing outside in your running gear, start walking and then maybe break into a jog. Movement leads to more movement—it's as simple as that.
- **Make It a Habit.** Doing this again and again turns it into a reflex. Over time, this Action Anchoring Technique can become a go-to move for getting past procrastination. It's about building a habit where your first instinct is to start with a physical action instead of overthinking.

Procrastination is a tricky beast with lots of different faces. What I've talked about here are five strategies that can help you build up your defences against it. But beating procrastination begins with a choice. The decision, as it always has been, is in your hands.

## Move Forward with Accountability

Acknowledging the battle against procrastination is a complex and enduring one, with no single strategy that can claim universal success. What works today might not work tomorrow. But if there's one thing that consistently helps, it's accountability.

You know how it goes. It's way harder to flake out on a gym session when someone is counting on you to show up. You're also less likely to let tasks slide into the abyss of "I'll do it later" when someone else knows you're supposed to be doing something. Suddenly, making excuses feels a whole lot less appealing.

Here's the thing about accountability; it's a dual-threat weapon against procrastination. First, it's a kick in the pants to get moving because nobody wants to be that person who always flakes out. Second, it's a bit of a cheerleader, celebrating your wins with you and acknowledging the rough patches you've navigated. When you vocalise your plans, they transform from thoughts into commitments with someone who will help you stick to them.

# III Boundaries: Shattering Limitations

You've heard about it, read about it, perhaps even preached it—boundaries are crucial. But figuring out how they function within our brains might just be as complex as deciphering the workings of gravity; always present but not so easy to explain.

This concept is frequently misunderstood as telling others what to do, however, boundaries are not just there to shield us from what others do. Rather, they safeguard us from our own emotional reactions and triggers. While we can't dictate how others around us behave, we do have the power to shape our responses, leveraging personal agency and insight. By establishing boundaries, we can help prevent ourselves from getting too stressed or upset by the actions of others, acknowledging all the while that their actions fall outside our control and responsibility.

This section of the book (Chapters 7 and 8) begins here, where we lay the foundation for understanding our limits through a neurological lens. We'll explore how the brain works to influence how we perceive and establish boundaries, setting the stage for real-life applications in the following sections.

In Chapter 7, the Bubble Up strategy is introduced as a metaphorical technique to carve out an emotional haven. This approach assists in safeguarding against external pressures and allowing for greater focus and mental peace in everyday life. It underscores the significance of self-care and setting boundaries proactively as a shield against life's inevitable dramas.

In Chapter 8, the discussion turns to communication. It provides practical language and strategies for communicating boundaries within your personal space. This chapter acts as a guide to improving spoken communication skills, enabling you to set and maintain your boundaries while focusing on genuine personal alignment.

Together, these chapters provide a toolkit for understanding, setting, and expressing boundaries. They give you the skills to deal with everyday challenges while protecting your emotional well-being.

But first, let's take a closer look at what happens inside the brain, and beyond, when we set boundaries.

## Boundaries: Inside the Brain

The way our brain sets boundaries is by always observing and absorbing information from everything we do. Whom we talk to, what we feel in certain situations, and how we react to the things around us. It takes all this data and starts drawing lines, much like a mapmaker, to guide us on what's good for us and what isn't. For instance, when we consistently find joy in certain activities or with certain people, our brain marks these as positive experiences. On the other hand, if something repeatedly makes us feel bad, our brain notes that too, suggesting we might want to keep those things at a distance in the future. It's like having an internal advisor who tells us when to proceed cautiously or when to open up.

The idea of the brain serving as an internal advisor becomes more apparent during times of being overwhelmed or feeling chaotic. Cast your mind back to a time when you were in a crowded place surrounded by noises and faces blending together. Amidst the commotion, your brain was silently carving out a peaceful zone for you, by filtering out unnecessary stimuli and concentrating on what was essential to make you feel safe and centred.

This flexibility, made possible by neuroplasticity, implies that your boundaries aren't at all fixed; they continuously adapt as you encounter individuals and navigate circumstances, enabling your brain to adjust your personal boundaries dynamically to suit your current environment. Whether an encounter prompts you to reshape your boundaries positively, or reinforces the importance of existing ones, your brain reacts, demonstrating its alignment with your needs and commitment to safeguarding your well-being.

When you notice that you are getting close to crossing these boundary limits, whether due to your own actions or the actions of others, your mind alerts you with a warning signal. These warnings usually come in the form of uneasiness, or a sense of discomfort, prompting you to either enforce your limits or reconsider them. It's all done in the name of protecting you, to prevent overwhelm by signalling when it's time to say no or take a step back for your well-being.

But have you ever thought about how we understand what others are thinking and feeling? The concept of *Theory of Mind* can shed some light on this. It's a psychological concept that helps us recognise that everyone has their thoughts, emotions, and reasons that differ from ours and that each person has their own inner world influencing their actions. By grasping this idea, we can connect with how others behave more empathically. This skill is essential for establishing and honouring boundaries in interactions. Acknowledging that there are differing perspectives allows us to set boundaries compassionately, safeguarding our well-being as well as promoting respectful and considerate relationships.

The amazing capacity of our brains to balance our personal needs with interactions is highlighted here in its effortless adaptation. This becomes especially important for those of you striving to maintain your inner balance while meeting your work demands.

## Boundaries: Beyond the Brain

Looking at this now from a philosophical perspective isn't only helpful in realising that boundaries truly do matter, but also in seeing the multifaceted roles they play in our lives. For instance, what wisdom would Lao Tzu, the great Tao father, bring into this conversation about setting boundaries? Well, perhaps he might wax philosophical, as he so often did, about the passage of time and the flow of life, comparing both to water—reminding us that rivers and streams cut through the rock with force, but also with grace. So, whenever we are carving out our own boundaries, we must do so with both strength and understanding. This viewpoint prompts a shift in our perspective, from drawing lines in the sand to influencing our exchanges with conviction and empathy.

Drawing on inspiration from the musings of Jean-Paul Sartre, this discussion gains even deeper insights. According to Sartre's philosophy of "existence precedes essence", our sense of self is shaped by the decisions we make, including how we define our boundaries. This thought-provoking argument challenges us to view borders not as barriers but as connections. While these boundaries may set us apart in some respects, they also have the power to bring us together and foster meaningful relationships with others.

The act of setting boundaries, then, is more than just taking up space. It also extends to managing your time between self-care and significant others. It's the same core idea that you find in Aristotle's notion of the golden mean, which advocates for a moderate, balanced approach to life rather than living in the extremes between excess and deficiency—and the Stoic message to practise only what is up to us. These time-honoured axioms place a premium, not only on boundaries as a tactic but rather as a discipline required for wellness and workable relationships.

How then do we navigate our walk on this tightrope of achieving this balance? It all starts with self-awareness, a concept also echoed by Socrates, who famously said "Know Thyself". It is crucial for us to understand our own needs as well as how they match or collide with the needs of others. As such, the exploration of boundaries becomes as much a philosophical undertaking as a scientific one, making us think about the subtle, almost invisible, powers according to which we move and counteract with the world around us. It asks us to walk the tightrope between the shadow and the light, engaging with society whilst savouring solitude, and balance with intention and grace.

In this section, we will discuss practical strategies for establishing boundaries that foster rather than fray connections. Mixing insights from neuroscience with philosophical viewpoints offers a revitalised perspective on an important skill for any motivated professional navigating today's complex social landscape.

# 7 | Bubble Up: Your Defence Against Life's Daily Dramas

**Figure 7.1   Strengthen Your Bubble Barrier**

**When to Use.**   You feel you need added protection from others' dramas and events happening around you.

During my time at a trauma clinic, I was constantly exposed to a whole host of emotions linked to fear and pain. It was here, against the backdrop of suffering, that I gleaned some of my most powerful life lessons that went beyond the usual suspects of empathy and resilience. Day in and day out, as I sat across from individuals grappling with trauma and addiction, it became starkly evident how crucial it was to safeguard my own psychological space. Through listening to these intense experiences in group therapy, I began to visualise everyone, myself included, moving about the room in our own personal "bubble". The bubble represents our internal world, and my role was to guide and support, but to do so from within my own bubble, and most importantly, not allow other people's experiences to infiltrate my bubble. It was quite an empowering shift in perspective earlier on in my career that profoundly reshaped how I would then go on to interact with my clients. Rather than shoulder their stories as burdens for me to carry, I began to view these narratives as bubble intersecting with mine, all while focusing on maintaining the sanctity of my own bubble.

This tactical move of establishing what I call *Bubble Boundaries* isn't about pulling back; it's about nurturing self-leadership, accepting responsibility, and ensuring independence. Of course, it isn't always comfortable; it entails making intentional decisions in steering your life by setting boundaries that prioritise what truly matters—your responses, where you put your energy, and the choices you make. Similar to a clinical environment, where emotional bandwidth is precious, in demanding working environments, every choice, interaction, and commitment can deplete your finite reserves of attention and energy.

The Bubble Boundaries strategy is indispensable for a reason. Research has demonstrated that having consistent boundaries leads to increased life satisfaction, reduced stress, and better relationships. Bubble Boundaries not only shield us from pressures but also help us understand our limits when it comes to dealing with other people's issues. Recognising that we cannot, and should not, carry the weight of others' problems is key. This understanding also extends to realising the impracticality of meeting every request, responding instantly to every message or engaging in everything asked of us. Learning to hold our boundaries allows us to help others, while also safeguarding our peace of mind, keeping us present to what really matters to us and steering clear of burning ourselves out.

## Four-Step Guide: Building Your Bubble

The Bubble Boundary you create isn't a product of your imagination; it actually acts as a shield that constructs a tangible defence against the various stressors that exist in your daily life. What helps me in considering where I need to set healthy boundaries is to ask what the best version of me would be willing to tolerate. Can I stand to be just a little out of my comfort zone? And what am I absolutely not willing to participate in? These questions function as a guardian for my well-being, allowing me to focus more on my interactions and actions towards others. Now, let's look at how we build this vital sanctuary.

### *Step 1: Recognise Your Personal Bubble*

Think of a personal bubble as an invisible force field that floats around you. It contains all your thoughts, actions, and feelings. It is as if every thought that you have had, every choice you have made, and every feeling you have ever experienced together make up this crystal floating sphere, essentially it's your inner world. This bubble is fluid and dynamic because it moves and changes in response to your needs. When you're at peace, it expands to welcome experiences that uplift you. Conversely, during times of stress or busyness, it contracts to focus all your energy and attention on what is important at that moment. Consider it an extension of yourself and one that influences how you manage the balance between your personal space and external demands.

Now flash to those times when everyone is vying for your attention, or your schedule is so packed that you can hardly catch a breath. Your personal sanctuary no longer feels as welcoming, does it? The bubble of space that usually surrounds you suddenly feels under siege from all directions. This intense pressure squeezes your space, making it smaller, tighter, and frankly uncomfortable. It's like this compression is pushing out the peace and comfort that usually reside within your bubble. The outcome? Your mood dips, your productivity may tank, and your interactions with others can become strained.

Getting a handle on how your bubble expands and contracts in response to the demands of your surroundings is the first step. This begins to explain why, on some days, you feel like you're effortlessly juggling every ball thrown your way, and at other times even the smallest disturbance can leave you feeling overwhelmed.

**Insight.**   The idea of your personal bubble is connected with how your mind understands limits. When your space feels threatened, it triggers your brain to switch into protection mode, increasing stress hormones such as cortisol. This response can create difficulties in establishing boundaries affecting both decision-making and emotional control. On the other hand, having a comfortable bubble size enables the brain to work at its best, fostering feelings of safety and contentment.

### *Step 2: Internal Forces that Shape Your Bubble*

Your bubble is like your own personal echo chamber tailored for you, where your preferences, aversions, convictions, and personal history reverberate. What influences it? It's a blend of your interactions; the principles that shape your choices and your perception of the world. Have you ever observed how effortlessly you click with some individuals while struggling to relate to others? Have you wondered why you're attracted to certain places but not others? Well, that's your bubble in action.

What's inside your bubble? From your successes to your setbacks and everything else in between. Each experience determines its character and shapes its essence. Understanding what's inside can help you see why you're drawn to particular choices or people. This process isn't just about identifying the ingredients of your bubble; it's also about understanding why they matter to you. When you do that, you're essentially mapping out your personal reactions and preferences, offering insightful reasons for what attracts or repels you.

Growing up in the United Kingdom, with parents who originated from India, greatly influenced how I navigated through most of my life. Standing out was actively discouraged. I needed to always blend in. Now, as you can imagine, this made it challenging for me to voice my opinions or assert myself. Consequently, I developed a skill for observing situations and adapting swiftly. Considering the well-being of others reflects the community-oriented values instilled in me during my upbringing. This encouraged me to embrace various viewpoints, albeit making me somewhat hesitant to prioritise my own needs and beliefs. Recognising the internal conflict that resided within my bubble is what eventually led me to build the skills to assert myself and take charge of decisions where I previously lacked confidence. What experiences have shaped your personal bubble?

**Insight.**   All the contents of your personal bubble are deeply connected with how your brain perceives your identity and sense of belonging. It is always trying to find patterns by sifting through experiences in the hopes of reinforcing your sense of self and where you fit in the world. That's why you might instantly click with people or things—they match the patterns your brain has learned to connect with familiarity and identity.

I am sure you will appreciate how having a varied mix of experiences in your bubble can help you think more flexibly, making it easier for you to adjust to new situations and viewpoints. On the flip side, if your bubble is less diverse it can be tough to step out of your comfort zone or see things from perspectives other than your own. By acknowledging and expanding what's inside your bubble, you grow personally. You also improve how you interact with a complex world where everything is interconnected.

### Step 3: External Forces That Shape Your Bubble

Your bubble is constantly vibrating with your daily goings-on. It absorbs fragments from each conversation you have, every swipe through your phone and every unspoken word. Identifying these influences is essential to keeping them in check and ensuring they align you with where you want to be.

Do you usually start your day by checking the news or social media first thing? It may seem like a part of your morning routine but can actually be like stepping into a storm of negativity. Without realising it, you end up sifting through doom-laden news and pessimistic posts, bringing a sense of stress into your day, under the guise of "staying informed". Compare that to the uplifting feeling you get from listening to your favourite music or an inspiring and funny podcast. Suddenly the combination of feel-good chemicals released in your brain, and the distraction from stressors, infuses your day with energy, raising your spirits for what lies ahead.

But the digital world isn't the only influence. Ever caught yourself in a cycle of complaining about everything under the sun with a co-worker or friend? What starts as harmless venting can quickly escalate into a negativity fest, fogging up your bubble before lunchtime. Or those never-ending marathon meetings that chain you to your chair, each passing hour polluting you with feelings of resentment which leech more and more light from your bubble. Setting up a no-fly zone for the stuff that eats away at your optimism is like saying: "This stops here. It doesn't enter my zone".

Tuning into the sway of these influences hands you the reins to shape your environment with intention. It's about identifying which interactions dim your sparkle and which ones polish it to a shine. Avoiding negativity is one thing, but actively selecting the influences you welcome into your bubble is where the real magic begins to happen.

Reflect for a moment—what's been pushing your bubble off its intended path? Are there changes you need to make to ensure it's being influenced more by what uplifts you rather than what weighs you down? For me, one example was deciding to only interact with social media after breakfast, and making a conscious decision not to start my day on a note dictated by the outside world. This simple boundary allowed me to control not just what news I took in, but when I engaged with it. I noted that my bubble became lighter and more buoyant; I started the day feeling more serene and ready to let the outside world in.

**Insight.** Your brain is constantly influenced by external factors, which can impact your flexibility to adapt and reorganise in response to experiences. Every interaction you have—whether online or in person—has the potential to strengthen some connections while weakening others. This process plays a role in shaping how you per-ceive things, feel emotions, and react to situations over time. Recognising the power of these influences empowers you to inten-tionally shape your surroundings, steering your brain's development towards the traits you wish to foster, such as optimism, compassion, and mindfulness.

### Step 4: Become the Boss of Your Bubble

"Keep your side of the street clean". Heard that one before? It's what we used to say back at the addiction clinic. It's simple yet packs a punch. Essentially, it means the atmosphere in your bubble—how you deal with life's curveballs—is totally up to you. Inside your bubble, you call the shots. What's outside, well, that's just background noise.

Here's how it works: kick to the curb of your street anything that's not in your control, like the soap-opera-level drama some folks (or even you) love to bring into your day. Next time drama knocks, hit the pause button and ask, "Is this my circus?" If it's not, then why buy a ticket to the show? Keep your bubble light and unclouded.

Before spending time with someone, take a quick pulse check. Do they make you feel charged up or like you're running on empty? If something feels off, it might be time to rethink how much room they occupy in your life. It's about keeping your peace front and centre, not giving the person the cold shoulder.

Now for the tricky part—dealing with those certain family members, co-workers, or bosses, who seem to have an all-access pass to your bubble. Unsurprisingly, the key lies in establishing clear yet courteous limits, and as always, a direct but kind approach works best.

I have always found it incredibly useful to have a few go-to phrases stored in my back pocket, ready for those moments when I'm caught off guard. For instance, if colleagues regularly interrupt you during a hectic day with issues that need your attention, you could respond by saying: "Thanks for letting me know. I just need some time to think about this. Can we talk about this [insert specific time/day]?" This approach shows that you are approachable and considerate while also giving yourself room to think and keeping your bubble intact. The aim is to establish a respectful distance without severing ties. In Chapter 8 we'll explore many more practical tips on how to set and convey these crucial boundaries with finesse.

But what about when you find yourself dealing with the aftermath of a difficult conversation? It can work wonders to do something small yet meaningful for yourself. Research supports this idea, demonstrating that simple activities like stepping out for fresh air, listening to uplifting music, or taking a moment to focus on your breathing can help change your body's response from tension to relaxation. These routines serve as both physical and emotional signals to your brain, indicating that it's time to move from a state of alertness and stress to one of peace and harmony. I find it beneficial to debrief with a close friend and permit myself to feel my feelings. This not only validates my emotions but also reinforces my resilience. Bottom line: you're the boss of your bubble. The company you keep and the energy you allow in are either going to darken and dull the inside of your bubble or make it clear and shine brighter. It all boils down to making those smart, albeit tough, decisions.

By actively filtering what comes into your life, you're doing more than just sticking to a routine; you're taking charge of your personal space. I'm not only talking about avoiding the bad, but also inviting in the good and making deliberate choices that shape a healthier and happier existence for yourself. Because living in a bubble isn't isolating yourself; it's about making sure your bubble is one heck of a good place to be.

**Insight.** The field of neuroscience highlights the significance of being the boss of your bubble, particularly when viewed through the lens of managing thoughts and emotions. By selecting what influences your bubble and responding thoughtfully to your challenges, you tap into your brain's capacity to regulate your emotions and reactions. Engaging in this process of understanding not only reinforces the connections linked to self-control but also decreases the activity in the amygdala, which is known as the brain's fear centre, resulting in decreased stress reactions. Ultimately, asserting control over your environment involves more than commanding personal space; it's a fluid journey that influences your brain's capacity to maintain a peaceful life.

### Case Study: When Boundaries Blur

When James shuffled into my office, he looked like he'd been through a war—totally exhausted from playing Mr. Fix-It for everyone else's dramas. Caught in a constant tug-of-war between two co-workers who treated him more like a carrier pigeon in their power struggles than a colleague, and at the same time trying to figure out single fatherhood with his two kids was, alas, only part of his battle. Add to that a fresh divorce and constant battles with his ex-wife over the minutiae of daily life, plus siblings locked in a cold war over inheritance money, and you've got a man whose life is anything but calm.

Each request from colleagues, friends, and family drowned out his own need for peace. James's coping mechanism? Play the peacemaker, zigzag through the drama landmines without getting hit. It might have seemed like the path of least resistance, but it was more like sticking a flimsy band-aid on a wound that needed stitches—it only left him even more drained. Reality was, James was barely hanging on, his daily anthem a dreary loop of "just get through the day".

The peace James longed for seemed like chasing a mirage. Without realising it, he'd turned into a lightning rod for stress and negativity, trapped in the middle of disputes that weren't his to solve—a story too many of us can relate to, right?

That's where our work kicked off. I introduced James to the idea of Bubble Boundaries—not just to build walls of protection, but to recognise where they were altogether missing in the first place.

James found it difficult to come to terms with the realities of his relationships and the unclear boundaries that tended to blur. Nevertheless, he saw a chance to carve out a space that was genuinely his own.

James began the "kick to the curb" process and distanced himself from negativity, guilt, and unsolicited demands. He taught himself to stop and question: "Is this truly my responsibility?" If the answer was no, well he kicked it to the curb. Obviously being accountable to me made it quite hard for him to revert back to his old habits. But, after a while, this shift in thinking became his guiding principle.

The first real test came when he found himself, yet again, sandwiched between the two sparring co-workers over a project mishap—a familiar spot where he'd typically play the peacemaker. However, this time James paused, armed with the insights gained from our discussions on safeguarding his peace of mind.

He explained to them that although he understood their frustrations, acting as the intermediary was not benefiting anyone, least of all himself. He suggested that they work together to resolve the issue or seek assistance from a third party. This was a respectful step, a gesture of help without overstepping his own boundaries. Over time, James found himself dealing with situations involving his ex-wife and sibling conflicts over family finances using a similar approach, with phrases that we would come up with together. So, instead of getting involved in the conflict, James utilised his boundary-setting skills by proposing direct communication between the parties involved, or seeking outside mediation when necessary. This action, assertive yet tactful, provided support without compromising his boundaries.

The aftermath? It was a bit of a mixed bag of reactions and some interesting revelations. At work, one colleague didn't quite see eye to eye with James's assertiveness, viewing it as rude and unhelpful. However, another colleague welcomed the push for a more direct approach. Although the situation didn't resolve overnight, James did begin to feel the burden of office politics slowly beginning to lift off his shoulders. Of course, not every boundary set by James was met with applause. There were times when people pushed back, misunderstood, or outright rejected them. The results depended on everyone's stress levels and schedules, including James himself. But these challenges did teach James an invaluable lesson; setting boundaries is a nuanced skill that can be messy, chaotic, and always demanding ongoing adjustment and determination.

This story doesn't just revolve around James; it reflects the challenges many of us encounter when navigating the realms of professional boundaries. The main takeaway? Establishing boundaries is a journey that requires mindfulness, bravery, and a readiness to confront circumstances—doing so from within your own bubble, and finding strength within yourself, is where true empowerment resides.

# 8

# Say It Right: Practical Language for Setting Limits

**Figure 8.1   Speaking Your Limits**

**When to Use.**   You need practical guidelines in setting limits.

"Set boundaries". It's advice we regularly encounter. Sounds straightforward, right? Yet, when you attempt to put this advice into practice, trying to convince your brain to get on board is where the real challenge lies.

But why is it such a dilemma for your brain? Neuroscience has some answers. Your brain, that complex machine geared for survival, often mistakes the act of setting boundaries for a potential psychological threat, even when it's a healthy and necessary action. This misperception kicks your fight-or-flight response into gear, placing you in an internal conflict over maintaining social harmony and self-preservation. Talk about a Catch-22!

So, what's the workaround? How do you convince your grey matter that boundaries aren't the enemy, but rather essential tools for your well-being and growth?

This chapter serves as your roadmap, packed with practical phrases to assist you in improving your boundary-setting skills. Many of my clients grasp the significance of setting boundaries, however, they often encounter challenges in articulating their needs while also considering others' feelings. Granted, it's a fine line. At times your efforts may come off as too forceful, while other times not sufficiently clear.

To bridge this gap, I've added some phrases that can help make things easier. The idea is to show you that setting boundaries isn't as tough as it seems. By giving you clear examples of how to set these boundaries, the goal is to shift the focus from being a source of stress to using boundaries as a support system, for staying healthy while maintaining respectful interactions.

## Guide: Setting Essential Limits

Let's face it, changing how you usually interact with people and their expectations is never easy. But then again, the best things in life rarely are. With that in mind, this section presents a hands-on four-step guide to assist you in laying out these essential limits.

### 1. Map Your Boundaries

The first, and perhaps most intuitive, step in setting up boundaries is to pinpoint aspects of your life that feel unbalanced. It's similar to diagnosing an issue with a piece of machinery; you can't fix the part that you don't know is broken. Here's a structured approach for doing just that:

- **Identify Intrusions.** Begin by taking a clear-eyed look at your day, week, or month to unearth stress triggers. Is work spilling into your personal time? Are your personal responsibilities overwhelming? Perhaps you're struggling to handle tricky people or challenging personalities, or certain people are asking for more than you can give, making you feel overwhelmed. Identify these sources of stress.
- **Limits Mapping.** Next, turn your attention to what about the certain tasks, responsibilities, or interactions left you feeling exhausted or upset. Maybe it was a conversation that didn't end well, a meeting that lasted too long, or a favour you felt compelled to offer but later regretted. These experiences serve as indicators showing where your boundaries may be lacking or altogether missing.

**Insight.** Mapping your limits activates numerous brain regions, including the hippocampus, which is important for navigation and spatial memory integration. This activity helps you picture your personal space and its limits while also reinforcing the elements that support self-awareness and self-preservation. As a result, your brain improves its ability to recognise and respond to violations of boundaries.

## 2. Straight Talk Wins

This section provides clear and assertive example phrases and strategies in Tables 8.1–8.7 to guide you in laying down the law effectively in professional settings, personal interactions, and managing your commitments—all while maintaining consideration for others. These phrases are straightforward and considerate, offering you a reference point to adjust according to your way of expressing yourself. Of course, I encourage you to personalise them to fit your comfort level.

**Table 8.1   At Work: Protecting My Time**

| | |
|---|---|
| **After-Hours Communication** | In order to enhance my productivity and start each day fresh, I'll be disconnecting from work-related communication after 7 p.m. Your support with this adjustment is greatly appreciated. |
| **Personal Breaks During Work Hours** | I plan to use my lunch break as personal time, so I'll be offline during that period. |
| **Creating Dedicated Work Blocks** | I've set aside blocks of time in my calendar with no meetings scheduled so I can focus on tasks without any interruptions. Thanks for your understanding. |
| **Promoting Planned Conversations** | Due to the complex nature of our projects, I plan to limit impromptu calls and prefer arranged meetings instead. This approach will help guarantee that our discussion is productive and well organised. |

**Table 8.2   Managing My Workload**

| | |
|---|---|
| **Juggling Priorities** | My plate is full at the moment. Adding tasks might compromise the quality of my work. Is there a way we can strategise on what needs to be addressed? |

| | |
|---|---|
| **Prioritising Key Tasks** | At the moment, I'm concentrating on tasks that directly support our team's urgent deadlines. As a result, there'll be a [insert time] delay in completing this task, please advise how you wish to proceed. |
| **Check-Ins for Agile Adjustments** | With the way our work is currently evolving, I propose we have a weekly meeting. This will help us quickly adjust if necessary and stay focused on our goals. |
| **Addressing an Immediate Request** | I understand the importance of this task and I want to give it the attention it needs. Given our priorities, could we perhaps plan to revisit this on [insert day] or explore the option of assigning it to someone else? |

**Table 8.3   Navigating Pushy Behaviour**

| | |
|---|---|
| **Respecting Personal Space** | I value our relationship. I'd appreciate some time to reflect on things at my own pace. I hope you can respect my need for a bit of space right now. |
| **Handling Overwhelm** | While I appreciate your enthusiasm, I'm feeling a little overwhelmed by the pressure. It'd really help me if you could be patient. |

*(continued)*

**Table 8.3**  (*continued*)

| | |
|---|---|
| **Seeking Respect** | It's essential that we respect each other. I understand your need for promptness. It's equally important for me to have my process and schedule honoured. |
| **Feeling Pressured to Share More Than You're Ready For** | I appreciate our chats and your curiosity about me. Talking about this topic isn't something I'm quite ready for at the moment. |

**Table 8.4   Dealing with Complainers**

| | |
|---|---|
| **Support Requirements** | Are you seeking advice, or simply wanting to vent your frustrations? Knowing your preferences can help me provide the support you're looking for. |
| **Recognising Emotional Expression** | I understand that sometimes all you need is to express yourself without any input from me. It's important for me to recognise that difference so I can be there for you in the way that suits you best. |
| **Handling Emotional Outbursts** | I sense there's a lot of emotions in what you are saying. It's completely normal to feel this way. How can I support you best while you work through these emotions? |

**Table 8.5 Handling Disagreements**

| | |
|---|---|
| **Respecting Different Opinions** | It's okay for us to have different opinions on this issue. What's important is that we respect each other's viewpoints, even if we disagree. |
| **Taking Time to Cool Off** | It seems like things are getting a bit intense. How about we pause for a bit to cool down? I'll come back to you this afternoon to pick up where we left off in the conversation. |
| **Seeking to Be Heard** | I value our discussions and think it's important for both of us to listen to each other without interruptions. For me, being truly heard and understood is more important than just "winning" an argument. |
| **Focus on the Issue at Hand** | Let's keep our discussions focused on the current issue instead of bringing up past arguments. This could help us find a resolution more easily. |
| **Use "I" Statements** | When sharing how I feel, I'll use "I" phrases so I don't come across as accusatory, because I want to keep our conversation constructive. |

**Table 8.6   Common Social Situations**

| | |
|---|---|
| **For People Who Don't Let You Speak** | Start by saying their name to get their attention, [Mark] can I share my thoughts on this? I have some insights that might add to our conversation. |
| **When Someone Keeps Interrupting You** | I really want to hear your thoughts; can I finish my thought first? |
| **When Someone Dominates the Conversation** | You seem really passionate about this topic, and I love hearing your thoughts! I'd love to contribute my perspective as well. |
| **When Conversations Become One-Sided** | I notice we've talked a lot about your experiences. Can I share something from my week? |
| **When Trying to Politely Exit a Conversation** | I've really enjoyed talking with you. I need to step away now, but let's catch up later. |
| **When Someone Assumes You Agree with Them on a Controversial Topic** | That's an interesting take. I actually see it a bit differently. Would you like to hear another perspective? |
| **Changing the Topic When Someone is Being Overly Negative** | It seems like this topic is really bringing you down. How about we find something more uplifting to discuss? |
| **When You Disagree but Want to Keep Things Friendly** | We seem to have different views on this, and that's okay. I appreciate that we can share and respect each other's opinions. |

| Staying on Topic During Conversations | Let's focus on key points in this meeting. It'll help me stay focused and make the best use of our time. |
| Engaging in Office Gossip | I see where you're coming from. I'd rather not discuss others when they're not here. |

**Table 8.7 Personal Commitments: Juggling Social Time and Well-Being**

| | |
|---|---|
| **Managing Last-Minute Plans** | I really enjoy spending time with you. To manage my schedule better I'll have to pass on any last-minute plans from now on. |
| **Cutting Back on Social Overbooking** | I've noticed my weekends are filling up fast, so I've decided to only book one social gathering on the weekends. |
| **Declining Requests That Conflict with Your Needs** | Currently I'm saying no to things that go beyond my capacity. It's not personal; it's just a way for me to take care of myself. |
| **When Encountering Unwanted Advice About Your Well-Being Choices** | I value your perspective and am currently following a plan that feels right for me. I'll definitely reach out if I want to consider other options. |

**Prepare to Disappoint Others.**   I totally understand that it can be quite difficult to set boundaries since the worry of letting others down can feel overwhelming at times. It's an all too common challenge to balance your needs with the demands of people that you value or collaborate with. Confronting this fear directly calls for more than comprehension, but a pragmatic approach that acknowledges both our boundaries and those of others.

If this doesn't feel natural, and it certainly didn't for me, consider easing into the setting of boundaries. Start by making adjustments that won't cause any disruptions or disappointments. For instance, if you're usually the go-to person for last-minute favours, consider turning down non-urgent requests or proposing an alternative time when you're available. This way both you and others can ease into your boundaries smoothly.

When getting ready to communicate these limits, it's important to be clear. Instead of saying something like, "I need more time for myself", it's better to explain exactly what you mean. You could say, "I'm committed to going to the gym on Saturday mornings". Being specific like this can make sure everyone understands and reduces any confusion. People also tend to appreciate your limits when they grasp the reasoning behind them. You don't have to elaborate. A brief clarification can help keep things smooth. Naturally, of course, there are also occasions when a straightforward "no" is all that's needed.

I find it goes a long way if you also recognise the emotions of the other person and provide them with some reassurance. For example, you could say, "I understand this may be disheartening. I do value our bond and want to make sure I can be fully present when we're together". This phrase communicates your thoughts with compassion while showing consideration for their emotions.

Preparation can certainly help ease discomfort. Practise how you'll communicate your boundaries. Rehearsing out loud, even if it's just to yourself in the mirror, can help you find the right words and tone before the actual conversation.

Finally, it's common to feel concerned about letting others down. It's important to understand that taking care of yourself isn't self-centred— it's vital. Whenever you establish a boundary, you're not just looking out for yourself, you're also showing others how to honour your requirements. Ultimately, this can result in fulfilling and equitable relationships where your needs are acknowledged and appreciated.

### 3. Stand Firm

It's important to have strong boundaries that aren't easily eroded, like sandcastles washed away by the tide. But as you know, establishing and upholding boundaries is anything but easy. The desire to not let others down, combined with the sheer dread of confrontation, only seems to add to the struggles of standing firm. Here are some practical tips to help you reduce the emotional burden:

- **Prepare Your Reactions.** To be ready for moments when you may feel uncomfortable, practise your responses with a friend or colleague. I've learned that having a plan in mind enables me to react calmly and confidently when the time comes.
- **Get Support.** Sending mixed signals by being firm one day and not the next can be confusing for others. However, this can be daunting, especially when the stakes are high, so make sure to seek out a trusted friend or ally who values your limits and can offer words of encouragement during times of uncertainty. Sometimes just knowing someone has your back can boost your confidence. Most importantly, keeping your boundaries consistent demonstrates to others that you are sincere in your words.
- **Reflect on Your Rights.** Reassure yourself that you are entitled to set boundaries. You have the freedom to say no to demands on your time and personal space and the autonomy to prioritise your well-being. Embracing these reminders can boost your resolve to maintain your boundaries.

Remember, staying true to yourself isn't about being inflexible; it's about helping you feel more grounded and fostering respect in your interactions.

### 4. Shape and Shift

Life is an ever-evolving journey, with your experiences and personal growth moving like flowing water. Therefore, it's only natural that your boundaries should, at times, be fluid too.

To demonstrate what I mean practically speaking, let's say you've made a decision to not work after 7 p.m. to protect your personal time. But suddenly you've been asked to spearhead an exciting new project that will require some evening collaboration. You might adjust this boundary to allow for flexibility on specific days and for a short period.

Or perhaps you have a personal rule to not lend money to friends in order to avoid the risk of straining your relationship. But if a dear and trusted friend suddenly faces an urgent financial emergency and has asked for your help, you may wish to adjust this boundary to support them during their time of need. Now, I am not someone who particularly likes making last-minute plans during the working week and prefer to keep a more structured schedule. But if I am invited by a friend to an important event or celebration, I often loosen this boundary to show my support.

In all these instances, to ensure consistency it's important to communicate any adjustments clearly and promptly with those impacted. This is important for preserving and honouring boundaries that can adjust to evolving situations.

Conversely, some boundaries should remain steadfast. For example, if you've established a communication rule with your partner to refrain from attacking each other's character while having difficult conversations, it's essential to stick to it to maintain trust and your sense of inner peace.

In order to help maintain alignment with your values and stay open to changes, where they may be needed, it's always worthwhile taking a few moments to regularly self-reflect on your boundaries. So, as you go about navigating the path of setting boundaries, consider this a gentle nudge: remember all the while that boundaries are not always fixed. They can transform like the waves of the sea, always adjusting and evolving with our life's ups and downs. So, keep an open mind, welcome curiosity, and above all always be ready to adapt your course as you gather perspectives.

In conclusion, the way I see it, when you establish boundaries with your words it sets off a chain reaction. The manner in which you converse with a colleague or a person at the service desk can affect how they engage with their loved ones down the line. Likewise, your interactions with children mould their communication with their friends. Your words carry weight for individuals you may never encounter again or who are unaware of your presence. This underscores the potency of communication as one of your tools for shaping others' perspectives.

## Case Study: Excelling Professionally While Struggling Personally

When it comes to dealing with personal boundaries, one client's story stands out. Jane. Her professional persona was a force to reckon with, the epitome of success and assertiveness. She could steer through boardroom challenges with grace, negotiate hard-hitting deals with unwavering resolve, and command respect effortlessly. But when the curtains fell and the spotlight shifted to her romantic relationship, the story took a surprising twist.

Have you ever experienced something similar to this? Doing well in your job, feeling self-assured and decisive at work, then feeling like things are a bit different once you're home and no longer in that professional mode?

If so, Jane's story could resonate more with you than you think. Even though she excelled in her career she often found herself going out of her way for her partner, neglecting her own desires and allowing her boundaries to become increasingly hazy. This led to a mounting sense of bitterness that loomed over her life.

It's almost ironic, isn't it? How we might be able to take charge of teams, handle projects, and hold our own in meetings, yet struggle to assert ourselves in our personal relationships?

For Jane, the journey to reclaim her boundaries was no walk in the park. It required her to enter new territory, such as voicing her concerns when her boyfriend made plans without consulting her. She was clever at hiding it too, telling me it wasn't a big deal or that she had bigger fish to fry. But once we removed the veil, it was a really big deal and far from straightforward for Jane; in fact, it actually marked a real milestone. It wasn't simply a case of saying "No this doesn't work for me" when her boyfriend unilaterally decided their weekend plans; it was about breaking years of silence bit by bit. Each phrase she mustered, like "I believe we should decide together" or "My opinions and time matter too" represented her self-respect. This went beyond communication; it was Jane reshaping the dynamics of their relationship in real time. These moments, though filled with vulnerability, represented a shift from the passivity that once characterised her life. They showcased her bravery and a move towards aligning her core values with reality, even if there were tremors in her voice as she voiced these sentiments.

You can picture the scenario. Her boyfriend, stunned at first with a puzzling look slowly beginning to creep across his face. Then, after pulling himself together, responding defensively, while Jane stands there, questioning if she had now just jeopardised her relationship over what some might consider a trivial matter. The anxiety about rocking the boat is real. It's not comfortable being labelled the "difficult" one after being the understanding partner for such a long time and detaching from this longstanding familiar dynamic.

Here's where things took a turn in Jane's story. Despite feeling scared, guilty, and constantly questioning herself (well, more like driving herself up the wall), she decided to stay true to her beliefs and honour her needs and wants; she discovered a little bit more about who she really was. You know what? Her relationship slowly transformed. Her boyfriend began to appreciate her, being more respectful and considerate of her wishes.

It's not just about Jane and her relationships. It's about all of us who have ever experienced the struggle between being strong at work and passive in our lives. Why do we quiet our voices once we leave the workplace?

Isn't it fascinating how our fears can sometimes hold us hostage, unable to go after what we really want? Isn't it empowering when we realise that expressing our needs can not only deepen our connections but also set us free?

Jane's situation is not uncommon; it mirrors a struggle many of us face. Juggling the roles we play both at work and at home brings up a question: Why do we often showcase our assertiveness in professional settings and hold back in our personal relationships or vice versa? Maybe it's about time to blend these two aspects, bringing our whole selves into every part of our lives. Ultimately, real empowerment comes from integrating rather than segregating our professional identities.

# PART IV

# Conflict: A Clash Course

Imagine for just one moment putting yourself in the shoes of students involved in the Stanford Prison Experiment, a notorious study conducted in 1971 by Philip Zimbardo on power dynamics. In this study, a university basement was turned into a prison where students assumed the roles of either guards or prisoners, which led to a situation characterised by abuse of power and dehumanisation. Because those playing the roles of guards fell into abusive roles, the prisoners swiftly adopted subservient behaviours, resulting in severe psychological distress. While this situation may seem extreme, it hammers home a crucial point; our behaviour can be significantly influenced by the roles we assume within the environments we find ourselves in, often resulting in conflict.

Now let's turn our attention to your life. You're always switched on, driven, and frequently dealing with disputes, whether at work, at home, or within yourself. While these situations may not be as dramatic as Zimbardo's experiment, they can nevertheless feel equally intense and demanding.

This begs the obvious question: How can you successfully manoeuvre through the tricky terrain that is conflict?

The Stoic philosopher Epictetus, I believe, said it best: "Men are disturbed not by things, but by the views they take of them". This proposes that it's often our perspective on conflict, versus the situation itself, that deeply affects us. When we look at conflict from this perspective, we start to perceive it not as an interruption but as an integral part of our evolving relationships. Those everyday disagreements? Maybe they are not just problems to solve but opportunities to rewire internal programming, overcome limiting beliefs, align more closely with our authentic selves and deepen our connections.

But have you ever wondered why you respond the way you do in difficult situations? According to neuroscience, our amygdala and prefrontal cortex play key roles here. The amygdala reacts quickly, by alerting you to threats and evoking instinctive emotional reactions. For example, you may feel your heart racing as your body gears up to handle the perceived threat, while the prefrontal cortex, responsible for thinking, takes a bit longer to respond. As a result, your emotions can sometimes override your logic during challenging situations, leading to the escalation of conflicts.

However, it's not only about how your brains are wired. Your own life experiences, personality traits, and societal expectations also play a role in determining how you deal with conflicts. For instance, experiencing a troublesome interaction with a colleague who criticised your work harshly in a team meeting can easily heighten your sensitivity. This makes you feel more on edge or defensive in future team meetings as your mind and body are on high alert to avoid being criticised or embarrassed again.

Having said that, there is reason for optimism because your wonderful brain can adapt by learning healthier strategies for handling conflicts. When you understand the relationship between your impulses, past encounters, as well as the potential for transformation, you can, with the right tools, more effectively address conflicts with a mindset that is more thoughtful and flexible.

This section begins by taking a look at the high-stakes world of hostage negotiation to uncover invaluable techniques for managing conflicts and building rapport in everyday interactions. The focus then shifts to mastering the art of assertiveness, providing strategies to express yourself confidently without compromising personal values or relationships. Finally, we consider innovative approaches to reframe complaints as powerful catalysts for positive change and growth.

We're certainly not going to suppress your emotions but rather learn how to handle viewpoints that differ from your own. Get ready for an exploration that mixes wisdom, scientific findings, and healing practices, and discover the many ways that you can handle conflicts with a thoughtful and flexible mindset.

# 9 | From Hostage to Harmony: Lessons from Hostage Negotiators

**Figure 9.1   Shift from Hostage to Harmony**

**When to Use.**   Resolving conflicts or diffusing tension.

In this world, every word holds significance and the stakes are incredibly high. But can you imagine navigating through situations where making a misstep doesn't just result in a deal falling through, it could mean life or death? Well, this is the daily reality for hostage negotiators in handling intensely pressurised situations. They understand human psychology deeply and their job is to create resolutions where, despite all the odds often being stacked against them, all parties can exit unharmed.

The insights I am about to share with you aren't lifted from textbooks or formal business courses. They stem from my eye-opening discussions with hostage negotiators. I've gotten a glimpse into their world where composure, strategy, and a remarkable sense of control are not just valuable but vital.

I had the privilege to spend hours having candid conversations with these negotiators, during which they shared the very real and raw reality of their highly pressurised roles. I was curious to learn how they stay composed when dealing with uncertainty, build trust during crisis talks, and steer situations towards peaceful outcomes. Despite the intense drama in their line of work, it became clear as we talked that their negotiation methods offer valuable insights for managing the conflicts that we face within our own lives.

You may wonder, why seek guidance from hostage negotiators when it comes to resolving everyday conflicts? The answer is simple; their success hinges on their ability to negotiate successfully in challenging situations. Their intensive training and practical knowledge have armed them with capabilities to stay unflappable in dire situations, build relationships with people in distress, and create situations where the results are universally positive. As we talked more, it became clear that the strategies they use in high-pressure negotiations are not just useful but also relevant to the less critical conflicts we face in our everyday lives.

The advice shared here is designed to equip you with actionable approaches for resolving conflicts that resemble your own high-stakes challenging scenarios. You too can learn the skill of negotiation, as demonstrated by experts who have excelled in high-stakes situations, and move more gracefully in smoothing out disagreements, recognising shared goals, and achieving results that benefit all parties involved.

## Guide: Applying the Hostage-to-Harmony Approach

Picture stepping into your next challenging workplace encounter equipped not just with your usual repertoire of coping skills, but with the composure and expertise of an experienced hostage negotiator.

This section presents a practical and adaptable guide that, while expertly developed in extreme situations, can be incredibly effective for handling everyday conflictual situations with confidence.

### Buy Time

In the early stages of a negotiation, a hostage negotiator's primary objective is to extend time. It's not just a delaying tactic; it gives them the space to thoughtfully plan their next steps instead of hastily making potentially risky choices. When faced with a client or colleague on the verge of losing it, your immediate response might be to react, whether it's defending yourself, getting into an argument, or trying to take control. This is your limbic system at work trying to keep you safe.

But rather than jumping in with quick fixes or defensive manoeuvres, the smarter play is to slow everything right down. Take a deep breath. This isn't just about calming yourself; it's about creating a pause for both of you. Use this pause to connect and convey understanding with something like "I realise this is very important so let's make sure we're on the same page". This approach doesn't just buy you time to think, it also begins to diffuse the situation by establishing mutual respect and a shared goal.

### Maintain a Poker Face

Now, just as a hostage negotiator enters a situation where emotions can run dangerously high, professionals in any field can find themselves facing emotionally charged confrontations. Keeping a composed demeanour, akin to a "Poker Face", isn't about concealing emotions, but rather a tactical skill deeply rooted in the practice of negotiating under extreme pressure.

When it comes to dealing with hostage situations, negotiators must maintain a sense of composure and avoid displaying any kind of emotion. Because showing emotion can inadvertently convey vulnerability, or worse still, escalate an already tense scenario.

Negotiators are trained to regulate their emotions, projecting a calm and collected demeanour amid chaos. It's not that the negotiators lack emotions but rather they manage them to maintain the stability of the situation.

We now turn our attention back to you. When it comes to dealing with your challenging workplace scenario, it's just as important to mimic this strategy and maintain your composure when faced with an upset colleague or client. The goal is not to ignore or push aside your emotions but to handle them more thoughtfully.

When you remain composed and respond by acknowledging the distress, for example, "I know this is [insert emotion] but let's try to work on finding a solution", you accomplish several objectives simultaneously. First and foremost, you affirm the other person's feelings. Moreover, you're also doing your bit to prevent potential conflicts from escalating. Lastly, you can then steer the conversation towards cooperation rather than confrontation. You can accomplish this by letting them know that you're committed to finding a resolution, and asking how you can tackle this together, which encourages a collaborative approach.

This method doesn't just calm the situation; it establishes a groundwork for a positive and problem-solving conversation. Like a hostage negotiator, employing the Poker Face tactic can help turn a potentially volatile situation into an opportunity for resolving issues and strengthening relationships, without the added drama.

### Stay Unflappable

In high-stakes hostage negotiations, the negotiator's ability to remain composed under pressure serves as a stabilising force. It's this composure that often convinces the other party to consider alternatives to their current course of action. The negotiator's calmness isn't just for show; it's a calculated effort to maintain control over the negotiation's direction without escalating tension or provoking further hostility.

When applied in a workplace context, embodying an unflappable attitude means leveraging your inner negotiator to navigate through conflicts or challenging discussions with grace and confidence. By acknowledging the situation and expressing appreciation for the other person's patience, as in saying, "I appreciate your patience as we navigate through this issue", you're doing more than just filling the air with polite words. You're signalling that you're in control of your emotions and, by extension, the situation at hand. This subtly communicates to the other party that despite the current challenges, there's a path forward—a path you're more than capable of guiding them along.

This strategy reinforces the idea that maintaining a calm and composed demeanour, especially when faced with opposition or high emotions, can effectively shift the dynamics of an interaction. It fosters an environment where constructive dialogue can flourish, and solutions can be jointly explored. By channelling your unflappability, you not only keep the situation under control but also open the door to resolving issues in a manner that respects all the parties involved.

### Echo Back

Continuing on, the Echo Back technique presents a nuanced approach to interaction that draws directly from the playbook of seasoned hostage negotiators.

During highly charged situations faced by hostage negotiators, they need to establish a bond with the person on the other side. One effective strategy they deploy is to mirror their language; this is, of course, to demonstrate that they're listening, but also to convey genuine efforts in understanding their viewpoint. It's a way of conveying, "I acknowledge your perspective, I value your thoughts. I am here for you". This can be disarmingly effective in lowering defences and opening up a channel for more productive communication.

Let's now put this into a real-life context. Imagine you are sitting in a meeting and someone has expressed their frustration or dissatisfaction towards you by saying, "This is completely unacceptable". Adopting the Echo Back approach involves responding by selecting a keyword from the conversation and repeating it to encourage further dialogue. So, you can respond with something like "I understand you think this situation is unacceptable, can you expand and tell me why?" This type of response achieves several things. Firstly, you acknowledge their feelings without passing judgement, showing that you respect their perspective. Next, it encourages them to go on and provide details, which can offer critical insights into their underlying issues. They also feel listened to and understood. Lastly, it changes the tone of the conversation from being confrontational to cooperative, creating a foundation for working towards a solution.

The concept of the Echo Back strategy goes way beyond repeating back words; it involves reflecting on emotions and viewpoints to create a space where transparent communication can pave the way for resolution and understanding. By applying this approach, you portray yourself not as an opponent but as a supporter in seeking an outcome where everyone is included.

### *Empathise Tactically*

This strategy brings in another aspect of the hostage negotiators' toolbox. It involves encouraging the other party to share their feelings, essentially giving them a chance to vent in a safe setting. Now, I'm not saying you need to silently endure their rant; think of it as tactically creating room for emotions to be expressed without criticism or instant pushback.

Hostage negotiators know all too well that when emotions run high it can lead to poor decisions, potentially making a bad situation even worse. By allowing individuals to vent their frustrations without interruption, negotiators avoid escalating conflicts with rebuttals or dismissive responses. Instead, they're recognising the human need to be heard and acknowledged. Once the initial outburst of emotion has passed, people are generally more receptive to dialogue and negotiation because they feel their emotional state has been acknowledged and respected.

In professional settings, tactically emphasising can be invaluable. When a co-worker or client seems visibly upset or annoyed, giving them space to vent without cutting in can really change how the interaction goes. Once they've had their venting session, simply acknowledge their frustration by saying "I get why you're feeling like this. Let's figure out how to improve things". This validates their feelings and also gently steers the conversation, from complaints to solutions, all without minimising or dismissing their concerns.

## Event Debrief

The *Event Debrief* strategy involves shifting your point of view to see situations not as obstacles but as opportunities to develop and gain knowledge. It's inspired by the attitude of hostage negotiators who, following tense negotiations, analyse their interactions to draw lessons that could improve future outcomes.

In the field of hostage negotiation, negotiators need to debrief and reflect on their actions. They carefully analyse the events that transpired, reflecting on their strategies, ways of communicating, and decision-making methods. Their goal is not to dwell on mistakes, but to recognise insights and chances to improve their skills.

Translating this into a professional setting, following a meeting or difficult discussion, you have the opportunity to turn setbacks into valuable lessons. By reflecting on what you can take from the experience, and considering how you might approach situations differently in the future, you are engaging in a positive self-assessment. This can take the form of writing down your thoughts and feelings about the interaction. This can help in organising your reflections and pinpointing specific areas for improvement. Alternatively, discussing the situation with a trusted colleague can provide new perspectives and insights, offering you support and possibly identifying solutions you hadn't considered. This practice helps you recognise both the strengths in your handling of the situation and areas of growth potential.

The Event Debrief acknowledges that every obstacle you face, regardless of how daunting it is, contains within it seeds of learning. This strategy promotes building resilience, flexibility, and a forward-thinking attitude towards your career advancement, oriented towards continuous learning and improvement.

Why not see each challenging encounter as a scene from a thrilling hostage negotiation movie? Picture yourself as the composed negotiator, leading the way with skill and composure, guiding emotions and conflicts towards constructive conversations and shared understanding.

By using these techniques you are not only solving disagreements but also honing your negotiation skills within the context of daily communications.

## Case Study: From Tension to Teamwork

I received an invitation to host a week-long workshop at a tech start-up known for its cutting-edge projects and intense work environment. The highly dynamic team often struggled with the complexities of navigating workplace disagreements, straddling the fine line between productive collaboration and disruptive conflicts. Among the challenges presented, the discord between the two founding members, Jordan and Sam, emerged as a particularly poignant example of how personal tensions can quickly escalate under pressure, also affecting the overall broader team dynamics.

Jordan and Sam were once seamless collaborators, but now it seemed they had hit a rough patch. It all began with a mix-up about who should handle a key aspect of the upcoming product release. However, as the deadline approached, this small misunderstanding escalated into major disagreements, leading to combative interactions, creating tension within the team that impacted everyone's spirits.

As their disagreement reached boiling point, it was evident that the usual ways of resolving conflicts wouldn't cut it. During the workshop we explored strategies to repair their deteriorating bond, drawing on the principles inspired by the skill of negotiating in highly charged situations. The objective was simple yet bold; change how they handle disagreements, converting moments of conflict into chances to strengthen their partnership.

We began by discussing the idea of taking a deliberate pause before responding to conversations. This simple practice required them to slow down their reactions, allowing room for thoughtful consideration amid the natural tendency to react defensively or argumentatively. As time passed, phrases such as "Let's carefully consider this" became more common than disagreements, leading to thoughtful and fruitful discussions.

During our discussions, we also paid attention to how each of their emotional expressions were handled. At first, both of them struggled to remain calm and maintain a composed demeanour, especially given their history. Yet, through practising an honest approach without allowing frustration to take over, they discovered how to steer their conversations in a more positive direction. Phrases like "I want to understand your perspective" served as a powerful tool for clearing up misunderstandings and signalled a commitment to resolving the conflict amicably.

When they listened to each other and validated each other's concerns, it was a part of moving towards reconciliation. Rather than preparing to argue back as the other person talked, they tried repeating what they heard by saying things like "So, if I understand correctly…". This not only showed that they were genuinely listening but also helped build empathy and respect that had been lacking in their conversations. Furthermore, giving each other the freedom to openly communicate frustrations without the worry of judgement or retaliation had a transformative impact. It wasn't an invitation to release stored-up grievances (we did that separately), but an opportunity to express thoughts in a controlled and respectful way. Beginning statements with "I need to share something on my mind" paved the way for conversations fostering openness and tackling root problems directly.

Through these subtle shifts in communication, Jordan and Sam started to repair their relationship. It wasn't an overnight fix. There were, of course, times when they regressed, but over time the foundation of their work friendship grew stronger and much more resilient.

Since our workshop I've been staying in touch with Jordan and Sam regularly, assisting them in implementing the strategies we came up with for the company at the workshop and addressing any obstacles as they arise. It's clear how dedicated they are to improving themselves, and the positive impact this has had on the company culture is remarkable, showcasing their evolution from strength to strength.

Their transition from conflict to collaboration served as a potent case study for the rest of the company, showing that even the most difficult relationships can improve with patience, mutual understanding, and effective communication.

# 10

# How to Be Assertive (Without Losing Yourself)

**Figure 10.1   Mastering Constructive Assertiveness**

**When to Use.**   In moments requiring effective communication and self-advocacy.

Assertiveness. It's often painted as the golden ticket in the professional world. Speak what's on your mind, ask for what you need, and don't easily back down; success is supposedly yours. But here's the thing, not everyone finds speaking up that straightforward. Do you sometimes catch yourself hesitating to share your thoughts? You're certainly in good company if you do. Many of us face a common battle, straddling the balance between a desire to maintain harmony and the fear of coming off too strong or stepping over lines. We're somewhat conditioned to blend in, and deviating from this—especially in a professional setting—can feel like you're swimming against a very strong current.

When my parents came to the United Kingdom from India during the late 1960s they believed that blending in was the key to success. In our home, speaking up for oneself was not only discouraged, it was openly considered a bad idea. Perhaps this narrative might resonate with some of you. Growing up in this environment, I didn't learn the skills I needed to express my thoughts and desires, in fact, what even were my thoughts and desires? So, instead, I became highly skilled at treading cautiously through life, always careful not to rock the boat.

Now, if I fast forward from this backdrop to instances when speaking up for myself was necessary, as you can imagine, this proved to be quite the challenge. Have you ever experienced the anticipation of sharing your opinions only to sense that your mind seems to have its own agenda? Just as you're about to speak with a well-timed thought it seems like your brain decides to sound the alarm, leaving you either at a loss for words or with muddled thoughts. This common scenario captures the conflict many of us confront; that tug of war between wanting to keep the peace and concerns about the reactions of the other party can make it exceptionally difficult to express ourselves when it truly matters.

Understanding the reasons behind your brain's reactions can also deepen your insight into the complexities of assertiveness. The brain's wiring plays an important role, especially when you find yourself in situations where you need to stand your ground. The amygdala (that's your emotion centre) can become highly active, leading to that familiar fight, flight, or freeze response, which isn't exactly helpful when you're simply trying to make a point during a meeting. Because your body will always prioritise this survival mechanism over thinking rationally, your prefrontal cortex (the part that's responsible for decision-making), now without sufficient resources, unfortunately gets side-lined. This can hinder your ability to articulate your thoughts effectively, so it's no wonder that asserting yourself can feel like an uphill battle.

Assertiveness is, of course, a behaviour that's extremely influenced by cultural and social situations. For instance, in some cultures being assertive is viewed as a positive trait, associated with someone who is a strong leader with clear and confident communication skills and effective in decision-making. But, in other settings, the same assertive behaviour might be considered rather aggressive, confrontational, or disrespectful, particularly if it clashes with values such as modesty or group harmony. This variation shows just how subtle assertiveness may be, influenced by cultural norms and expectations on expressing your demands and ideas.

If you've ever felt invisible during discussions, or maybe found yourself on the verge of being too forceful, you'll know all too well how tricky a line it is to walk, feeling like you're either not heard or being too much.

However, becoming more assertive isn't just achievable but also incredibly empowering. Thankfully you don't need to become the loudest person in the room or dominate the discussions. It is more about discovering your voice in a manner that is authentic, respectful, and impactful. This chapter aims to assist you in understanding the subtleties of assertiveness. By putting these strategies into practice you'll not only bolster your self-confidence but also enhance your ability to positively influence those around you.

But first, let's take a moment to consider the various communication styles that exist around us. Recognising the distinctions between assertiveness, aggression, and passivity—and comprehending their significance—can give you the edge when it comes to harnessing the true essence of assertiveness.

## Exploring the Kaleidoscope of Communication Styles

You can think of the various ways we communicate existing along a spectrum. Assertiveness occupies a position around the middle, avoiding the extremes of being overly forceful and hostile on the one end and excessively timid and submissive on the other. Kind of like the Goldilocks zone of communication. Here are some of the most common communication culprits:

- **The Bulldozer.** It's as direct as it sounds. So, at one end of the spectrum, we have those people who plough through with their agenda neglecting others' perspectives. This type of communicator can be quite forceful in ensuring their message is heard but it often comes at a price. It's a hollow victory when you completely lose sight of the bigger picture, ultimately driving people away and hindering overall progress in the long run.
- **Silent Struggler.** At the opposite end of the extreme, we have the passive communicator. This is somebody who tends to take a back seat, rarely expressing their thoughts or desires, and consistently allowing others to take control. They may believe they are maintaining harmony but in reality, they are marginalising themselves. This position is far from ideal and frequently results in growing sensations of annoyance, powerlessness, and sometimes even stress.
- **Covert Conflict.** Being caught in the middle of a conflict can also be just as tricky. This person might come across as friendly on the surface but inwardly is actually feeling anything but. They agree openly but inwardly are secretly pushing back through subtle actions of defiance like delaying tactics, being stubborn, or purposefully working inefficiently. While it may seem like a way to sidestep arguments, this behaviour often leads to confusion and frustration, preventing a genuine resolution from emerging.
- **Assertiveness.** Now, this is the sweet spot somewhere in the middle. It allows you to express your thoughts and desires without stepping on other people's toes or being completely overlooked. It's maintaining that mix where everyone's views are respected and appreciated. Mastering assertiveness means finding a way forward, forming strong connections, and keeping your sanity intact. I mean, who wouldn't aim for that?

Understanding where you currently stand on the communication spectrum is, of course, an essential first step. Now that we've identified some of the most common communication pitfalls, let's now turn our attention to exploring the truly transformative part; actionable techniques for enhancing your assertive style.

## Guide: Mastering Assertiveness

Entering the world of assertiveness may not always be such a breeze; it is, however, certainly within reach. If you're accustomed to environments or mindsets that tend towards passivity, aggression, or passive aggression rather than assertiveness, honing in on these aspects can greatly assist you in discovering and upholding a balanced approach.

The following ten tools can help you traverse the tightrope of being healthily assertive, without falling into aggressiveness or passivity.

### *The "Yes, And" Technique*

The great debate of using "but" versus "and" might seem like splitting hairs, but honestly, this can turn a dead-end conversation into a super-highway of thoughtful exchanges.

Let's have a chat about the word "but" for a moment. It's quite a sneaky little word, isn't it? It always shows up just when you feel like you're making progress in a conversation. "I understand your point but" and all of a sudden it feels like everything said before the "but" vanishes into thin air. Your excellent argument disappears in an instant! This can often result in misunderstandings cropping up in the blink of an eye.

The "Yes, And" technique is actually derived from improv theatre, where performers use it to build narratives collaboratively, and it's quite a useful tool for those wanting to communicate more effectively. It involves acknowledging someone's perspective ("Yes") and then smoothly incorporating your thoughts or needs ("And"), encouraging a more expansive and productive conversation flow. So, the next time you're about to use the "but" bomb in a conversation, try using "and" instead. It might just be the magic touch your discussion needs to turn it from dull to scintillating. Table 10.1 provides a few examples to showcase how effective it can be.

**Table 10.1   The "Yes, And" Technique**

| | |
|---|---|
| **Expressing Concerns to a Manager** | I'm grateful for the opportunity to lead this new initiative **and** I'm also concerned about balancing this with my current tasks. Can we discuss what support might be available or how we might rearrange existing priorities to make it more manageable? |
| **Disagreeing with Your Partner** | I totally get your wanting to spend the holidays with your family **and** I also feel it's important for us to start creating our own traditions. What if we mix it up by taking turns each year? |
| **Dealing with Conflict** | I see why you thought that decision was best at the time **and** I feel we might have missed some of the implications. Let's go over them together to come up with a plan for the future. |
| **Differing Opinion from a Co-Worker** | I see the value in your idea **and** based on what I've seen trying out this other method could also improve our outcomes. Why don't we test both and see how they compare? |
| **During a Negotiation** | I get the constraints you're working under **and** I believe we can find a win–win arrangement by adjusting some of these terms. Shall we explore some other possibilities? |

| | |
|---|---|
| **In Client Meetings** | Yes, the features you've highlighted are essential **and** adding these additional functionalities could set us apart from competitors. Would you be open to discussing this further? |
| **Handling Feedback** | I take your points on board on how the project was managed **and** implementing a different strategy could prevent similar issues in the future. Can we set up a time to discuss these improvements? |

Using the "Yes, And" technique is priceless in any setting where communication and creativity are key. This approach allows you to show your understanding and willingness to be open, while also expressing your requirements and ideas cooperatively.

## Drafting a Rehearsal

Before that really important conversation you know you need to have, it can be helpful to jot down your thoughts, requests, or boundaries in draft. Yes, it helps organise your thoughts, but this small action is also giving your brain a nod signalling it to prepare for that moment of truth. When you take the time to write out your thoughts, you're doing more than just preparing; you're participating in a dynamic conversation with your mind.

The fascinating part is the science behind it. When you write, it activates various parts of your brain. It's not just that you're putting words down; you're also beginning to link them together, forming associations and creating pathways that assist in recalling the information. Essentially, you're constructing a bridge in your mind, which makes it easier to transition from thought to speech, which is pretty useful when you need it most.

But there's also more. This rehearsal isn't just a mental exercise—it's a stress reliever too. Ever noticed how laying out your outfit the night before an important event eases your mind? It's the same principle. By organising your thoughts beforehand, you're cutting down on the mental scramble during the actual conversation. This clarity doesn't just make you more articulate; it dials down the anxiety, making room for confidence to take the stage.

It's a bit like rehearsing for a show but in your head. It helps you when the moment comes because you're not just prepared but gaining confidence and ready to nail it. So, when there's something at stake, remember the importance of getting prepared. It's not just smart; it's neuroscience.

### The Rule of Three

Limit yourself to making three key points. In meetings or negotiations, use this strategy to help you stay focused and assertive without overwhelming yourself or the audience. It forces you to prioritise your arguments, amplifying the impact of your words.

> The **Rule of Three** is a principle that suggests that things in groups of three are more effective, memorable, and satisfying than other numbers. It's a concept that's been used in many forms of communication for centuries, including storytelling, art, photography, and rhetoric.

Steve Jobs, the visionary behind Apple Inc., famously applied this rule during product launches, highlighting three main features or benefits that set his products apart. This approach revolutionised tech marketing, showcasing that assertiveness blended with simplicity can indeed leave an indelible mark.

This principle is also mirrored in the world of storytelling, where authors leverage the Rule of Three to structure narratives with a beginning, middle, and end, creating a satisfying rhythm for the audience. Such a structure ensures the audience's interest throughout, proving that a focused approach can significantly enhance engagement and retention.

Adopting this strategy in your communications enables you to present with more authority, engage your audience effectively, and ensure your key messages resonate and endure. The Rule of Three isn't just a technique; it's a pathway to more impactful and assertive communication.

### Embrace the Power Pause

In the professional world, assertiveness isn't just about what you say, but also about how and when you say it. The Power Pause is a brilliantly simple strategic tool in this regard. By intentionally pausing before you respond, you not only give yourself a crucial moment to gather your thoughts but also project confidence and control. This pause can be particularly effective in meetings or negotiations, where the pressure to respond swiftly is high.

However, embracing this pause can be easier said than done, especially when you're facing a stressful situation. A couple of subtle ways to buy yourself a little time might be to ask the participants a thought-provoking question to engage their minds while you take a brief pause, perhaps invite questions from the audience, or share a light-hearted comment. One practical tip I often use is to use the moment to take a sip of water. My very first corporate public speaking engagement was at none other than Google, which invited me to share my entrepreneurial story. No pressure, right? Anyway, I had rehearsed my presentation to within an inch of my life, but as you all know, when you're thrust into the spotlight anything can happen, so having a "power pause" anchor helped re-centre me.

The natural action of sipping water not only gives you a brief interval to collect your thoughts and structure a response but also serves as a physical reminder to slow down. It also demonstrates that you are not reacting impulsively but are in control of your thoughts and actions. It elevates your interactions by signalling that your contributions are considered and deliberate, thereby commanding respect and attention in any setting. Just make sure you have a glass of water handy for such situations!

### Transform Interactions with "I" and "I Wish" Statements

Being someone who enjoys making others happy, using this tool was both difficult and freeing. It made me more aware of my emotions. It also encouraged those around me to do the same. Incorporating phrases like "I" and "I wish" has completely changed how I communicate, letting me be genuine and confident, without coming off as aggressive.

**"I" Statements for Assertive Communication.** Using "I" statements is really effective in sharing how you feel and what you believe without pointing fingers or accusing others. This method focuses on you expressing your own feelings and experiences. A common way to express yourself using "I" statements looks like: "I feel [emotion] when [situation] because [reason]. What I'm looking for is [solution]". This slight adjustment can change the whole trajectory of your discussions. Here are some examples:

- Instead of saying: "Why don't you ever wash the dishes!" try "I feel frustrated when I come home and find a pile of messy dishes because I want to come home to a clean space. I'd like us to work on it".
- Try replacing: "You are always late!" with "I feel disrespected when you show up late because my time is very valuable to me. I want us to use our time well together".

This approach helps to diffuse potential tension by focusing on how the actions of others affect you and seeks to find solutions rather than assigning blame.

**"I Wish" Statements to Soften Delivery.**   When expressing your needs or boundaries in a softer manner, using "I wish" statements can provide a gentler approach. Presenting your thoughts as wishes allows you to convey your perspective in a manner that's more respectful while remaining straightforward.

For instance, saying, "I wish I could take on that project, however, my current workload is at capacity" effectively communicates your limitations without a direct refusal.

"I" and "I wish" statements are both highly effective tools for conveying your needs, feelings, and boundaries. These approaches not only enhance your assertiveness but also build bridges of understanding and cultivate cooperation, making them invaluable for gracefully navigating interactions.

### Schedule Assertiveness

Often, my clients don't know where to begin when practising being assertive. An easy place to start is leveraging your regular touchpoints, like those weekly team updates or monthly one-on-ones with your boss, as opportunities to practise asserting yourself. This way, you're not adding more to your plate; you're simply making the most of the meetings already in your calendar. Turn these moments into opportunities to communicate your needs, goals, and boundaries with clarity and without the need to carve out additional time from your already packed day.

### The Feedback Sandwich—Remixed

While the feedback sandwich method (positive–negative–positive feedback) is well-known, let's remix it for assertiveness by starting with appreciation, introducing your need or boundary and closing with a collaborative question.

For example:

- "I'm grateful for your quick turnaround on tasks. Moving forward, I could use some help with figuring out what to focus on when everything feels urgent. How can we collaborate to establish these priorities?"
- "Your guidance on these projects has been amazing. To make sure I'm meeting expectations I'd appreciate feedback on how I'm doing. Could we schedule a time to chat about this in detail?"

This approach balances clarity with respect while maintaining a positive tone. It's about being clear and open without coming off as too harsh or passive.

### Accept You Can't Dictate Other People's Behaviour

Avoid taking the blame for other people's reactions to your assertiveness. If they respond with anger or resentment, strive (hard as it may be sometimes) to refrain from reciprocating in a similar manner.

Just keep at the front and centre of your mind that you can only manage your own actions and reactions, so try to remain composed and thoughtful when situations become intense. As long as you're being considerate and not infringing on someone's boundaries, you have the freedom to express yourself however you see fit. Here are a few ways of handling negative responses:

- "It seems like my feedback may have made you feel uneasy. My intention was to enhance our work process and not to criticise you personally".
- "I feel that things are getting a bit intense and I want to work this out without letting our emotions get the better of us. Perhaps we should take a short break to cool off?"
- "I feel you may have interpreted my directness in a way that wasn't what I intended. I'd love to hear your thoughts so we can work together positively".

Each of these statements recognises the emotions of the other person without attributing fault to their responses, highlighting a dedication to constructive dialogue and mutual consideration.

## Stick to the Facts

During difficult discussions, things can sometimes get a bit intense and veer way off track. To maintain a civil dialogue while expressing your viewpoint, try to spotlight the facts presented in front of you instead of allowing emotions to lead you into guessing the other person's intentions.

In keeping attention on the facts, you focus the conversation on things that can be handled at that moment and work towards solutions that benefit everyone. At the same time, keeping your focus on what you know to be true also helps minimise the negative emotions that can arise from speculating about another person's motives.

Here's an example:

- **Emotional Speculation.** "We noticed you didn't contribute during the client call. It seems like you're not trying to engage with the team".
- **Sticking to the Facts.** "I observed you were quiet during the client call today. I understand we all have different comfort levels

in meetings. Let's discuss how we can support you in feeling more prepared and confident to share your insights next time".

## Body Talk

According to research conducted by behavioural psychologist Dr. Albert Mehrabian, a whopping 55% of how a message is received depends on our body language.[1] The way we hold ourselves during communication often speaks louder than words alone.

Think of your body as a silent narrator, telling a story without saying a single word. This narrative can dramatically shape the way your verbal messages are perceived and received.

Enter the idea of "body talk"—a term I'll introduce to describe the art of using body language to boost confidence and engagement in conversations. So, just how do you master this art and transform every interaction into a captivating dialogue, all while not having to say more than is necessary?

- **Stand Tall.** You know how superheroes strike their poses, well there's a purpose behind their stance. Standing with your feet solidly on the ground and your shoulders squared (without the cape, naturally) doesn't only convey confidence to onlookers; it initiates a series of shifts in your body, elevating your self-assurance. It's not about appearing assertive; it's about experiencing that feeling from within.
- **Speak with Your Eyes.** Mastering the subtleties of eye contact is a skill. A fine balance must of course be struck. Too little can convey disinterest, while too much can feel intense. To perfect the skill of "eye talk", focusing on maintaining a welcoming gaze can help emphasise key points in your discussion. More concretely, just enough time to note the person's eye colour is a good amount of time. Think of it as highlighting your spoken words, which adds depth and authenticity to your

---

[1] Mehrabian, A. (1972). *Nonverbal Communication*. Abingdon: Routledge. https://doi.org/10.4324/9781351308724.

message. Kind of like how you use the bold and italic functions in Microsoft Word to add weight to your sentences.

- **Speak with Your Hands.** Our hands are expressive tools that can bring life and depth to our words. Instead of crossing your arms or leaving them motionless at your sides, use them to emphasise your ideas and direct attention. A well-timed gesture can serve as a visible underline of your statements, ensuring that your message sticks with the audience. Confident gestures not only complement what you say but also convey a sense of self-assurance and clarity.

- **Draw Them In.** The act of leaning in during a conversation can be likened to saying, "I'm all ears to hear what you're saying". This gesture not only shows engagement but also prompts the speaker to share, openly strengthening the bond with them. It's an action that carries weight, transforming passive listening into an active involvement.

When you start to see your body language as a core aspect of how you communicate, you can become a much more engaging and persuasive speaker. It's not only about getting your words across, it's about really feeling heard on a whole new level. So, the next time you're chatting with someone, keep in mind that your body language speaks volumes—and it has some pretty compelling things to say.

# 11 | Complaint Conversion

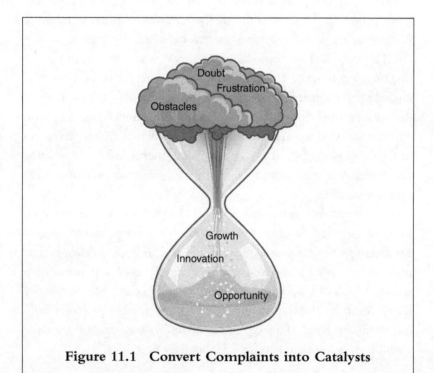

**Figure 11.1  Convert Complaints into Catalysts**

**When to Use.** Whenever you're dealing with constant complainers.

My days at the rehabilitation clinic were anything but dull. It was a place filled with a mix of people each facing their own unique challenges and eccentricities. Some of them tended to complain a lot, using it as a distraction from addressing issues—like throwing smoke bombs to create clouds of confusion in our conversations. Yes, it could get pretty intense, and let's just say I got quite the masterclass in handling constant negativity and turning it into something constructive. It is where I refined the art of turning sour grapes into fine wine.

Navigating a flood of grievances often felt as tricky as threading a needle, especially when my own energy levels were dwindling. I'll be honest. The usual woolly self-help advice—with its highfalutin principles and clichéd expressions—sometimes felt like I was bringing a knife to a gunfight. That's why I have opted to ditch the small talk and get down to brass tacks with what I've dubbed the *Complaint Conversion* tactic—a straightforward no-frills approach for tackling negativity head-on.

This approach is rooted in gritty, real-world lessons from the therapy trenches. On the one hand, the principles of positive psychology served as my secret decoder tool, helping me look beyond the surface-level complaints and discover the underlying strengths and unexpressed desires in each issue. The aim is not to cover up problems by slapping on a happy sticker, rather it involves reshaping the problem to uncover forward-thinking resolutions that benefit everyone involved.

On the other hand, stoicism served as a compass during turbulent times, urging me to concentrate on the things within my control. Embracing a Stoic attitude also meant I had to double down on my patience, understanding, and effective problem-solving prowess. It revolved around the central question: "Right, what's my next move here?", even when faced with a sea of complaints and problems from the clients in rehab. This change in focus enabled me to prioritise resolutions rather than getting consumed by negativity.

## Guide: Convert Complaints into Catalysts

The three-step Complaint Conversion approach is more than a theory. It's a set of battle-tested tools tailored for anyone who has ever been overwhelmed by complaints, whether at work, in relationships, or, like me, when dealing with the challenges of a therapy clinic. Let's dig in and get ready to turn those sour grapes into the finest wine.

### Step 1: Cracking the Complaint Code

It took me a long time to realise that when people complain to me, they have a need that needs attention. So, before taking a plunge into the unknown, let's take a moment to figure out a plan that will keep the both of you from feeling like you're swimming against this current. How about throwing out this lifeline to them: "Hey, do you need some advice right now or do you simply need me to lend an ear?" It's like finding the key for a lock without having to test each one on the keychain. If all they want to do is vent, well done! You've just become the Chief Listening Officer.

Now, your mission, should you choose to accept it, is simple but crucial: tune in and listen with the intent to understand where they're coming from, not just waiting for your turn to talk (something I used to struggle with). Empathise and let them unpack all the burdens they've been lugging around. Arm yourself with some go-to phrases, such as:

- "Oh no that sounds really tough, I'm here for you. What happened next?"
- "I can totally understand why that's bothering you. I'd probably feel the same way".
- "It's completely okay to feel unsettled by this and I'm here for you".
- "Tell me more".

It's not only about conserving your energy; it also closes the gap between you into a comforting refuge where concerns can be discussed without the urgency of instant answers. It's like being calm in their storm, guiding them towards a lighthouse without having to fix the weather.

### Step 2: Dishing Out Empathy and Advice

Alright, suppose they have offloaded and are ready to want to listen to your thoughts. Great, now it's your moment to speak but keep it simple. Consider your reply as a clear direct line; begin with empathy—smoothly insert your advice in the middle—and conclude with understanding.

It could look something like this: "I can tell this is really affecting you…" establishes the right tone. Next up, offer your advice, keeping it simple and practical. Lastly, remember to end by recognising their difficulties with a phrase such as "dealing with a problem like this can't be easy".

Here's another example of how you might plate this up:

"I understand the pressure you're feeling. What about trying [insert recommendation]…? I know it's a lot to handle, but I've seen you tackle tough stuff before".

Or:

"That seems like a lot to handle [insert recommendation]… It's normal to feel overwhelmed at the moment. How can I best help you?"

The objective here isn't to sugar-coat things or skirt around the issue. You're letting them know that you're paying attention and empathising, while also giving support and actionable advice they can use.

### Step 3: Turn Those Grumbles into Gold

Let's now turn our attention to how you can shift complaints into opportunities. Here's the game plan for turning those venting sessions into chances for development.

**Constructive Spin.**   Approach every complaint as an opportunity for positive action. For instance, if someone is venting about how they're swamped with tasks, you could say "It certainly sounds like you have a lot on your plate. What's one small adjustment that could ease your pressure?" Notice the shift? We've transitioned away from acknowledging the stress into triggering a moment of insight where they begin thinking about solutions.

Now, if someone approaches you all wound up with frustration over another person's behaviour, here's a smooth move: "It seems like [person's name] knows exactly how to get under your skin. Have you thought about how you'd like to handle that, for the sake of your sanity?" By framing it this way you're prompting them to take charge in finding a way to address the situation or make adjustments. The key is encouraging personal agency in resolving their problems in any situation.

**Listening Without Losing Your Spark.** When someone is venting, they usually look for an understanding ear. However, it's equally important to keep your own spirits up too. Set yourself a mental limit on how long you engage in venting conversations, especially from someone who views it as a national sport (yes, we all have that one friend!). Then smoothly transition to a different topic, much like a magician's skilful redirection. Here's an example: "That reminds me of an article I came across. Have you heard about [topic]? It's quite intriguing". This subtle move demonstrates your engagement while gently steering the conversation towards a more sparky subject, for both of you. Think of it as attentive listening with style; fully acknowledging where they're at while gracefully guiding the discussion towards a more light-hearted note.

**Constructive Confrontation.** When you've exhausted all your go-to moves but the complaints keep on pouring in, it could be an idea to change your approach and just be honest with them. Address the issue directly by sharing how the constant negativity is starting to weigh heavy on you. The trick here is to talk about your own feelings rather than accusing them of their behaviour. It's not about assigning blame; it's about creating a window of opportunity for introspection and potentially prompting some changes.

You could say something like, "Hey I've noticed our conversations are leaning towards the negative side lately and I'll be honest, it's leaving me feeling quite drained. How about we also try to find the sunshine in our conversations more often too?"

We are all aware that persistence plays a role in the process of turning complaints into efforts. Real progress takes time and requires patience without losing motivation. The goal is to slowly transition towards a vibe that's more focused on progress than frustrations.

If you still find yourself overwhelmed by emotions it might be an idea to step back from people, social events, or gatherings that bring you down. You could also try creating a mental space for yourself to find peace amidst the chaos, as discussed in Chapter 7. This mental sanctuary is not about isolating yourself from the world but prioritising your well-being. Remember, you're simply considering their perspective without compromising yourself. Setting this boundary can help you stay calm and authentic no matter what challenges come your way.

# V | Turning Stress and Worries into Wins

Are you feeling stressed or is it more of an anxious feeling you're dealing with? If you sometimes struggle to identify which emotion you're feeling, believe me, you're not the only one. Getting through your days with your sanity intact pretty much hinges on being able to tell the two apart. No, it isn't just about slapping labels on your feelings; it's about unlocking a deeper understanding of what drives them. By understanding this, you can come up with a game plan for confronting each one head-on. Why does this matter? Well, because knowing whether you're facing a fleeting challenge or a lingering worry can totally change how you tackle the problem. So, let's start with understanding how these emotions show up in our lives.

Imagine stress as that friend who pops by unannounced, gets you all riled up for a bit, but leaves as soon as the fun's over—similar to that feeling you get when you're racing against a deadline or bracing yourself for a tough chat. This type of reaction is short and sweet (not exactly sweet but you know what I mean), providing a sudden boost of energy and focus that diminishes once you've dealt with the issue, allowing you and your body to relax and get back to normal.

Anxiety, on the other hand, feels a bit like that family member who dropped by for a weekend but ended up extending their visit indefinitely on your sofa. It's a state of ongoing worry or unease even when there's no immediate crisis, that doesn't necessarily tie back to any one event or situation. With anxiety, even after the race is run, your heart's still pounding and your mind's caught in a loop of endless "what ifs" and worries about the future.

For those of you who are always on the move, it's important to first and foremost recognise and tend to your most basic needs. Remembering HALT when you feel Hungry, Angry, Lonely, or Tired helps you tune into your brain's signals. Feeling hungry triggers your survival instincts; anger can ignite your fight or flight response; loneliness connects with your nature; and tiredness signals the need for rest. By acknowledging these states and addressing them head-on, you can communicate effectively with your brain in its own language, restoring equilibrium and improving your decision-making abilities. So, the next time stress or overwhelm creeps in, take a moment to HALT, pay attention to what your brain's trying to tell you, and respond thoughtfully. This simple practice can lay the groundwork for distinguishing between stress and anxiety while guiding you towards effective ways of managing both.

Getting this distinction isn't just nice to have—it's essential. While jumping into action can help ease stress linked to specific issues, anxiety, which has its roots in more general worries, often needs a different approach, one that might involve changing how you think and react over time.

In my line of work, I've met plenty of folks who dismiss mindfulness practices like meditation, despite its known benefits. "Who has the time for that?" they ask, looking at their schedules sceptically. That's where therapy steps in to lend a hand, providing an expedited, down-to-earth approach to untangle those worries.

In Chapters 12 and 13, I'll be sharing various metaphoric techniques that I've found to be effective and easy to follow for coping. By blending neuroscience, timeless wisdom, and proven therapy methods, we'll map out a tailor-made plan for you to not just get by the tough times, but change how you handle stress and anxiety in a practical way.

This, of course, is not about guaranteeing you a life free from troubles—sadly no such miracles here. Instead, it's about equipping you with the skills to ride life's ups and downs with a bit more grace and a lot more self-assurance. Drawing from a wealth of personal and professional experiences, I've witnessed first-hand how adopting a strategic approach can transform problems into catalysts for personal evolution.

# 12 | Balloon Strategy: Release Your Worries

**Figure 12.1   Balloon Your Worries Away**

**When to Use.**   Whenever things beyond your control weigh you down.

When it seems like you're holding onto too much, then trying out the *Balloon Strategy* could just be what you need. There have been many times in my life when uncertainty didn't come knocking on my door; it barged right in unannounced. Taking that leap of faith of leaving the structured corporate world to the great unknown of entrepreneurship felt more like a plunge into freefall than a gentle step into uncertainty. Submitting that resignation letter was both terrifying and exhilarating in equal measure. Doubts flooded my mind, with questions such as "What do I do now?", "Am I making a monumental mistake?" These thoughts were constant echoes feeding into a growing sense of self-doubt and anxiety.

It was during my time interning at a clinic that I came across the Balloon Strategy as part of a group therapy session. I had no idea that this simple practice of releasing control would become such a revolutionary way to face the unknowns within my own life. I'm excited to now pass on this invaluable technique to you, especially if you constantly find yourself in unfamiliar situations without a clear path forward.

Whenever you face highly pressurised situations, your brain tends to go into overdrive, whether it's dealing with deadlines or simply the uncertainty of what lies ahead. It's as if it's gearing up for a battle you can't see. This response isn't limited to changes; it happens whenever you stress yourself out or anxiety kicks in. What's interesting is how neuroscience explains this; when stressed, the amygdala (your brain's alarm system) takes control over the prefrontal cortex (your thinking centre), which goes on the back burner. This shift can turn every molehill into a mountain and coat every decision with a layer of anxiety. Your brain is essentially magnifying the perceived threat, sending your emotions into hyperspace.

To understand better, do you know about something called the *Law of Reversibility*? Well, if not, this principle suggests that changing what we do can alter how we feel. The Balloon Strategy therefore isn't simply a metaphor; it's an approach rooted in neuroscience. It utilises this law by prompting you to participate in the process of *releasing* your concerns, thus recalibrating the equilibrium between your feelings and logical thinking. In essence, it involves taking measures to handle stress and worries directly impacting your emotional state through your actions.

A fun fact to add to the mix is that the human body can't differentiate between physical and psychological stress. When your body responds to stress—whether the source is physical (e.g., running a marathon) or psychological (e.g., managing tight deadlines)—the physiological response is largely the same. This means that techniques like the Balloon Strategy, which helps reduce stress in your mind, can actually help make you feel better physically too.

Now, it's time to explore how you can reclaim control, one balloon at a time.

## Guide: Applying the Balloon Strategy

The Balloon Strategy works by imagining every worry as a balloon. You can decide to either cling to it, adding to your burden, or release it and lighten your load. It's particularly useful when you're feeling highly emotionally charged but still need to keep it together and remain focused and efficient. Here's how you can turn those pesky unwanted intrusions into blips on your radar, keeping you unflappable and on-point.

### Step 1: Identify Your Balloons

Think of each worry as a helium balloon. Seeing your worries as something separate from you begins to reduce their impact; that is, you are not your worries but the observer of them. You can even pick a colour for your balloon that reflects your mood. For instance, you may choose blue, representing a mix of worry and doubt, and label this balloon "Worry Doubt". Giving it a name is another strategic move towards weakening its control over you.

Now carefully evaluate if there is an action you can take to ease the concern. If a feasible solution is within reach, then proceed to outline actionable steps, or enlist someone to help you out. On the other hand, if the problem is beyond your control, or cannot be resolved promptly, it is essential to acknowledge this limitation and prepare yourself mentally to transition into the next stage.

### Step 2: Understand Helium's Role

If you reflect on the helium's ability to remain buoyant, it acts as a kind of symbol for lightening the load of your emotional burden. This perspective blends insights from neuroscience and ancient Eastern wisdom which emphasise the fleeting nature of emotions. Recognising the brain's natural tendency to fixate on negativity (the heavy stuff) allows you to then make the conscious decision to release these thoughts. Now, visualise trapping your feelings of "Worry Doubt" into the worry balloon; this step is priming your mind to release these emotions, paving the way towards relief and mental clarity.

### Step 3: The Release Mechanism

Opting to set free the balloon signifies your choice to shed the weight of these burdens. Reflecting on Newton's First Law serves as a reminder that much like physical objects, our thoughts also linger stagnant until we take action upon them. Practically speaking, I confront these lingering anxieties with a statement of release, such as: "I don't know what to do with you, so I choose to let you go" and surrender the helium balloon (encasing my emotional burden) out to the universe, or God, or whatever resonates with you, remembering all the while you are relinquishing control over that which is uncontrollable. Watch the balloon float away carrying with it your mix of worry and doubt. Witness its departure up into the ether carrying away the weight of your troubles and begin to embrace the feeling of an emerging sense of relief, from knowing that it's okay to let go of this weight to focus on what matters right now.

### Step 4: Watch the Balloon Ascend

As you watch the balloon ascend higher, with each deep inhale and exhale breath you have a chance to cleanse your mind, letting go of any residual negativity of "Worry Doubt". This act of releasing is more than shedding weight; it serves as a ritual to purify both your thoughts and soul, demonstrating your dedication to maintaining emotional stability and a sense of groundedness. You believe that whoever or whatever you've entrusted your balloon to in the unknown will handle what you can't control at this moment.

### Step 5: Repeat as Necessary

It might become apparent that oftentimes this exercise of releasing needs to be done daily or even multiple times during the course of the day. The real benefit lies in how simple the method is and how easily it can be integrated into your schedule. Participating in this regular routine begins to fortify neural pathways, boosting your ability to bounce back from challenges and reducing the intensity that comes from encountering unforeseen stressors.

Consider it a form of gentle emotional alchemy, where the weight of negative feelings is transformed into lighter, more manageable states, ready to be set free into your mental sky. With continued effort, what starts as a momentary release slowly blossoms into lasting resilience and adaptability.

## Case Study: Anna's Journey Towards Self-Liberation

Anna was in her thirties, carrying a lifetime of stories in her eyes when she walked into my clinic. Stories of an upbringing where volatility and uncertainty were the norm and emotional wounds ran deep. Her early years were marked by a struggle, not against a visible enemy, but against the dread of setting off her mother's unpredictable temper.

Fast forward to adulthood; those childhood scars had turned into what felt like a constant need for approval. We referred to it as *Approval Anxiety*, not just to give it a fancy term but one that captured the essence of her experience. For her, every conversation felt like navigating a minefield, every interaction an exam she might not pass. Her days were consumed by the pursuit of approval, leaving little space for her authentic self to shine through.

Introducing the Balloon Strategy didn't magically erase Anna's anxieties. It did, however, set her on a journey towards confronting them. The idea was simple yet challenging. See her anxiety as an entity separate from herself, place the troublesome thoughts into the imaginary helium balloon, and observe it drift away. Sounds easy enough, doesn't it? Well not quite. To Anna, this exercise sometimes felt like trying to separate pages stuck together with superglue without tearing them. At times her anxiety felt too overwhelming for any balloon to carry away.

Despite facing daily struggles and being completely fed up with old habits, Anna persisted. She envisioned herself letting go of each balloon, feeling her worries loosen their grip with every release. She also sought comfort in reciting her soothing mantra, "I now release you and trust all will be well", alongside taking deep breaths, to gain a sense of calmness in the turmoil of her thoughts.

Anna's journey is, of course, a continual one. Because there are still moments when past fears resurface, casting dark shadows over her path. However, she now has in her possession a resolve that has been built from her unwavering dedication. The Balloon Strategy has emerged as her trusted tool of choice, allowing her to confront and release approval anxieties gradually. Today she explores life outside the realm of seeking approval. The journey is challenging with its ups and downs, but she's making progress by letting go of the past, one balloon at a time, as she goes. Each step is a testament to her strength, a declaration of her independence from her past.

If you're going through a particularly uncertain time, like Anna, keep in mind that making a difference doesn't always mean taking monumental actions. Sometimes a small and visual approach can help you break the cycle of anxiety.

# 13 | Traffic Light System: Don't Speed into Stress

**Figure 13.1 Tackle Stress One Signal at a Time**

**When to Use.** When life throws a curveball and stress levels are rising.

Let us now dive into the exciting world of stress (hmm… said no one—ever). Nevertheless, it is a topic that needs attention and I can't find a more relatable way to approach it than by likening your stress to a traffic light. But don't break a sweat because I won't now take you into a detour through roadworks. Instead, I want you to reimagine these light signals as your stress level checkpoints: Green (Keep Going), Amber (Caution), and Red (Stop). Here's a no-nonsense practical guide to handling stress, one signal at a time, for someone as driven as you:

- **Green Zone (Keep Going).** Here you're in your element; you know, where everything feels second nature and you're operating in cruise control. But don't get too comfortable; it's a zone for performing not growing.
- **Amber Zone (Caution).** This is where you feel your mettle is tested, and challenges are beginning to pop up, pushing you out of the comfy lane. It's time to switch gears and channel all that nervous energy you're experiencing to take the necessary action to evolve.
- **Red Zone (Stop).** You've taken a wrong turn and ventured into dangerous territory! When stress takes control over the wheel it can be an all-consuming force poised to push you off the road into the pit of burnout, so it's time to make that emergency SOS call for backup. Consider this a warning signal to stop and recalibrate.

Contrary to the widely held misconception, stress isn't necessarily this sinister force that's quietly plotting your downfall. Because it can also morph itself into a powerful motivator. When properly harnessed it can be used as the fuel you need to drive you towards your personal and professional milestones.

Let me just clarify one thing, the objective here isn't to get rid of stress—that's an endeavour as futile as it is misguided. Think of the *Traffic Light* strategy not as rules to follow, but as a helpful dynamic guide that lets you channel the energy generated from stress into something constructive. I know what you might be thinking, "OK, but how can I transmute this theory into an achievable reality?"

## Guide: Applying the Traffic Light Strategy

To begin, get into a habit of regularly asking yourself: "What colour zone am I currently in?" This straightforward inquiry can help you acknowledge your current state and where you need to be headed.

Now that you've identified your zone, roll your sleeves up because the real work begins.

### Play in the Green Zone

It's tempting to peg the Green Zone as simply a comfortable place to pause, catch your breath, and enjoy a respite from life's hustle. However, it also offers more than a time-out; it's a laboratory for self-development and discovery.

Here, in the calm, you can set the stage for your next big leap. It's an opportunity to contemplate, evaluate, and plan without being in the pressure cooker environment of stress.

You could think of the Green Zone as a playground, a place where you can freely explore your creativity. Here without the fear of failure looming over you, you have the freedom to dream bigger, learn new skills, and challenge your limitations. In this tranquil environment, you can confront obstacles that might appear overwhelming, turning the quiet into a catalyst for growth and discovery.

### Manage the Amber Zone

Whenever you find yourself in the Amber Zone, it's like you're fast approaching a fork in the road where you need to choose to travel towards either the route of distress or determination:

- **Ditch of Distress.** You know this path, everything seems intense, leading you to react defensively, impulsively, or feel completely out of your depth.
- **Determination Highway.** Here, you know you are being pushed to your limits but not beyond. You also know growth and development await you just up ahead.

Choosing which route to take isn't simply a matter of willpower; it's about technique. One effective, albeit unconventional, approach is engaging in third-person self-talk. Let me explain. Instead of affirming myself by saying "I can do this", I tend to switch gears and address myself as if speaking to someone else: "Jay, you have overcome 100% of the hurdles life has ever thrown you, and you have what it takes to overcome this obstacle. No matter what, you will grow through what you go through, so let's go". Yes, it feels strange at first, but this practice mirrors advice often given by sports psychologists to elite athletes seeking to break free from negative cycles. This simple and immediate shift helps create a separation between you and the stressor, allowing access to a deeper wellspring of self-confidence and strength that lies beneath.

Science also backs this up, drawing from the concept of *Self-Distancing Theory*. This theory proposes that viewing oneself in the third person, when facing stressful situations, can better help you manage your emotions and actions. It's like stepping outside of yourself and assuming the role of a mentor, offering yourself the backup needed to be able to confront the challenges that lay ahead of you.

Keep in mind, however, that even the most capable amongst us can't remain in the Amber Zone indefinitely. It's important to give yourself the opportunity to recuperate and get back to your Green Zone. Failing to do so may lead you down a path towards burnout, entering the dreaded Red Zone.

### *Steer Clear of the Red Zone*

In order to steer clear of the dangers of veering into the ditch of distress, it's important to act decisively. Here are five quick and easy life-saving tools that serve as emergency brakes helping you find your footing again.

**1. Find the Ground with 5 4 3 2 1**    When your stress levels begin to feel uncontrollable, indicating a high level of distress, it is crucial to take quick and decisive action. One immediate strategy you can tap into is the "5 4 3 2 1 Grounding Technique".

Here's how it works:

5: Take note of and name five things you can see around you.
4: Recognise four textures or surfaces that you can feel.

3: Listen carefully and identify three sounds.

2: Identify two scents in the air.

1: Acknowledge one flavour that you can taste in your mouth.

Here's why it works. By getting all the senses involved, you are cleverly redirecting attention away from the confusion caused by stress towards the calm of the present moment, which helps reduce the grip of stress. Similarly, you could listen to music and sing along to the lyrics or read out loud the words you are reviewing on a report or document. Your brain will struggle to stay focused on the problem while you're simultaneously doing something else. It's a method supported by research drawing on mindfulness and cognitive psychology principles, providing a path to regain mental equilibrium.

**2. Get into the Circle of Calm**  Every so often during your stressful day, give yourself the gift of a 360-degree outlook. Stand up, slowly turn around, and observe your surroundings with a gentle gaze. This exercise is about engaging your peripheral vision, moving away from the tunnel vision that computer screens often force upon us. This simple act can coax your brain out of the cycle of stress, guiding your nervous system from a state of alertness to a more peaceful and relaxed state. Why not give it a spin during your next break? You might be surprised how this mini-physical break gives you a quick mental reset and helps break the cycle of rumination. It may even inspire a few curious glances, providing a perfect opportunity to spread those calming vibes around the office!

**3. Employ the 20–20–20 Rule for Digital Strain Relief**  Similarly, and because your digital life can tether you closely to your desk much longer than is healthy, the 20–20–20 rule is a simple yet effective countermeasure to combat visual fatigue. Every 20 minutes, redirect your gaze to something 20 feet away for 20 seconds. This not only gives your eyes a chance to relax and refocus but also gives your mind a much-needed break, helping to disrupt any accumulation of stress.

**4. Transition into Box Breathing**  Life is a series of transitions. Utilise the moments when you transition from one task to another—walking to a meeting, waiting for a document to print, or even while your computer wakes up. These transition times are perfect to practise *Box Breathing*, which gets its name from the fact that you divide your breathing into four steps as if you were breathing along the four edges of a box. I love this strategy because you can use it without breaking stride in your day:

1. Inhale for a count of four
2. Hold for four
3. Exhale for four, and
4. Hold for four.

Engaging in this method soothes you by engaging the parasympathetic nervous system, which is responsible for rest and relaxation. When you practise this breathing technique consistently, you signal your brain to transition from a state of heightened alertness (fight or flight) to a state of peacefulness and rejuvenation (rest and digest). This shift leads to a decrease in heart rate and blood pressure, which contributes to creating an overall sense of calm. The rhythmic nature of box breathing also helps reduce stress hormones, making you feel more relaxed and centred. This method is also used by US Navy Seals, who frequently find themselves in high-pressure situations, where keeping a composed and focused mindset can often mean the difference between life and death. Through the practice of box breathing, they can control their stress levels, enhance their clarity, and excel in extreme conditions. It's a powerfully simple tool for managing acute stress on the go.

**5. Apply the 5-Year Rule**    Lastly, and one I use all the time on autopilot, is reframing thoughts with the 5×5 guideline. If it's not likely to matter in 5 years then it shouldn't occupy more than 5 minutes of your focus in the present. It's so simple that it's often dismissed. But the reality is that so many of the things we worry about are temporary and not worthy of excessive concern. And thinking of it in this practical way leverages your brain's decision-making capability by reducing unnecessary stress. Taking a beat to zoom out and observe the problem from a broader perspective can help you rationally refocus your attention on what is truly important. This approach is based on cognitive behavioural therapy (CBT), which promotes a shift in viewpoint, thereby reducing the impact of stressors.

Steering clear of the Red Zone doesn't call for piling more onto your already full plate. While there are many techniques available that can help you, these tailored strategies are designed to blend seamlessly into your day-to-day activities, guiding you back to a state of calm in real time without slowing down.

As we conclude our discussion on stress management, it's important to recognise that dealing with stress is only one piece of the puzzle when it comes to looking after our emotional well-being. In the next section, we'll explore the concept of understanding and dealing with those pesky negative thoughts. By mastering the art of steering through and reshaping these thoughts, you'll find yourself better prepared to nurture a healthier outlook. These will perfectly complement the stress management techniques we've covered here and further contribute to strengthening your ability to bounce back with resilience and grace.

# PART VI

# Conquering Negativity

When your world seems drenched in fifty shades of grey, and your inner voice is never happy, it's clear we've all bought tickets to the same show—The Chronicles of Pessimism. But this isn't just any performance; it's a universally shared experience, where our darkest thoughts take centre stage in our minds. But what exactly gives these thoughts the power to take the limelight in our consciousness and captivate us? Let's briefly turn our attention to neuroscience and philosophy to unravel this mystery.

Peering through the lens of neuroscience we find that negative thoughts are not just abstract concepts; they are processes happening in our brains. The spotlight falls on our prefrontal cortex, often referred to as the brain's "control centre", which plays a role in regulating our thoughts and feelings. But in times of stress or anxiety, the body's fight-or-flight centre (aka the amygdala) takes over and redirects the brain's resources to more primal survival responses; stirring up feelings of fear, increasing stress hormones, disturbing the balance of neurotransmitters, weakening cognitive functioning, and impairing the process of memory formation.[1] All of this happens at the expense of the rational thinking of our brain's control centre, turning our mental landscape into quite a turbulent theatre of emotions.

You could think of your brain as a weather station which has been carefully calibrated to favour thunderstorms over sunnier skies. This phenomenon, fondly known as *negativity bias*, means that your brain is better at spotting lightning bolts than rainbows. This feature was a hit in times of prehistoric survival shows, helping our ancestors to evade dangers like sabre-toothed tigers. In today's world, however, it feels more like wearing tinted glasses that paint everything with a shade of pessimism.

Travelling eastwards, we also find age-old insights softly whispering timeless truths. For example, Buddhism introduces the concept of *dukkha*—the sense of unease stemming from our struggle with reality.[2] Viewing negative thoughts through this lens, they appear as the tantrums of the mind, upset when events don't go according to the storyline we have scripted.

Similarly, Taoism explores the balance between Yin and Yang, highlighting the harmony that exists between the contrast of darkness and light—how darkness defines the light; relating this to our negative thoughts, they also find a place within our positive thoughts. This philosophy highlights the duality and interdependence of these opposite forces, seeing our negative thoughts not as adversaries but as vital cast members in our theatre of life.

Fast forward to today and contemporary thinkers such as Jean-Paul Sartre confront negative thoughts more directly by urging us to take responsibility for the feelings that arise from the immense freedom of determining our own paths.[3]

Drawing from this rather eclectic blend of brain science, ancient teachings, and contemporary ideas, it's clear that pessimistic thoughts

---

[1] Arnsten, A.F.T. (2009). Stress signalling pathways that impair prefrontal cortex structure and function. *Nature Reviews Neuroscience* 10(6): 410–422. doi: 10.1038/nrn2648. PMID: 19455173; PMCID: PMC2907136.

[2] Stanford University (2018). *The Buddha (Stanford Encyclopedia of Philosophy)*. Last modified June 21. Available at: https://plato.stanford.edu/entries/buddha/.

[3] Stanford University (2016). *Jean-Paul Sartre (Stanford Encyclopedia of Philosophy)*. Last modified July 21. Available at: https://plato.stanford.edu/entries/sartre.

are deeply ingrained in who we are, shaped by the pathways in our brains, the wisdom passed down through generations, and our philosophical reflections. Yet despite this predetermined script, we find our agency. While a storm of thoughts may swirl uncontrollably within us, we can still direct the drama that is our reactions.

Chapters 14–17 in this section are dedicated to arming you with strategies to engage with your negative thoughts in a way that builds resilience, nurtures mindfulness, and turns your everyday challenges into sources of strength.

# 14

## Worry Window: Time-Box Your Troubles

**Figure 14.1  Time-Box Your Worries**

**When to Use.**  When negative thoughts cloud your focus or feelings of overwhelm take hold.

Michael Jordan, often hailed as the greatest basketball player in history, had a remarkable talent for compartmentalising. He excelled at leaving any of his doubts and fears outside the court, making sure they didn't affect his game. This mindset enabled him to maintain laser-focused concentration and engagement from one moment to the next and game after game.

Similarly, the principle behind the *Worry Window* mirrors this disciplined approach. It involves recognising your concerns and worries, but not allowing them to interfere with, or overshadow, your productivity in tasks and objectives. It champions the idea of dedicating a specific time each day to address them and then gently shelve any remaining disconcerting thoughts. I appreciate this might feel like a tall order but might I also remind you how powerful you are? Contrary to how it might feel sometimes, you do have power over your thoughts. I've worked with so many people stuck in the pits of anxiety for years on end and once they truly grasp that they possess this insane ability to choose their thoughts; well, it changes everything. I can't think of a better way to showcase this ability than by dedicating yourself to time-boxing your worries.

This method serves a dual purpose. Firstly, it anchors you in the present, ensuring you stay fully concentrated on the task at hand. Secondly, it confines your worries to a designated time, thereby preventing them from seeping into and dominating your day. Much like Jordan's approach on the basketball court, where negative thoughts were not permitted to undermine his performance, the Worry Window provides a structured mechanism to manage worries effectively.

But how does this method, which seems at first glance to invite negativity, actually work? Insights drawn from science on the concept of thought suppression offer some clarity. Research suggests that oftentimes when we try to suppress our negative thoughts it only causes them to come back with greater force, much like trying to throw a boomerang in one direction.[1] Setting a specific time to engage with these thoughts helps to decrease their frequency and intensity over time.

---

[1] Wegner, D.M., Schneider, D.J., Samuel, R. et al. (1987). Paradoxical effects of thought suppression. *Journal of Personality and Social Psychology* 53(1): 5–13.

This approach isn't about indulging in negativity, but about recognising that these thoughts exist and creating a structured way to address them without the constant tug of lingering worries. Ultimately, adopting the Worry Window strategy can help you regain clarity and command over your mental space amid the daily grind, allowing you to concentrate on moving forward with purpose and resilience, much like Michael Jordan did on the basketball court.

## Guide: The Worry Window

This approach not only helps manage your negativity; it effectively buys back the time otherwise lost to it. Here's how to incorporate the Worry Window into your schedule, transforming lost time into time gained.

### Step 1: Schedule Your Worry Window

Think of it as a meeting with your mind, perhaps a brief 10 to 15-minute rendezvous each evening. Personally, I like to carve out this niche right before wrapping up my workday. Aim for a time that is far enough from your bedtime to avoid disrupting your sleep.

### Step 2: Gather Your Gloom

As you move through your day, capture those pervasive intrusive negative thoughts as they arise by jotting them down or making a note on your phone. This act is not about avoiding them, but rather seeing it as a way to address them more purposefully with intention and reflection later on. What I like to do is acknowledge my dark thoughts, when they arise, by saying (in my head) something like, "I see you and I know you're important, but I will reflect on you during my Worry Window at 6 p.m.".

### Step 3: Shift Your Spotlight

Once you've noted down your worries it's important to shift your attention back to the present. But if you're struggling with thoughts that just won't loosen their tight hold over you, try acknowledging their weight by telling yourself "This feels heavy, but it sits here on this notepad for now, not within me". Remember that these distractions have their place and time separate from this present moment. Repeatedly taking this step can reduce their intensity, giving you the space to concentrate on the task or moment in front of you.

### Step 4: Tackle Your Worry Window

With your Worry Window now open, it's time to start sorting through that list. Taking a moment to really think about each worry tends to shrink them down to size. Frequently, you'll discover that the concerns that seemed overwhelming earlier have now become more manageable or disappeared entirely. For those that still weigh heavy, figure out a small action or two you might take towards beginning to face them. And for those worries you can't do anything about, but they still weigh heavy on your soul, think about giving the Balloon Strategy (mentioned in Chapter 12) a go—allow them to float away.

### Step 5: Wrap It Up When Time's Up

When your dedicated time slot is up, it's time to close the Worry Window. Any thoughts that didn't get resolved? They're on pause until your next session. Then, ease back into your day with a clearer head.

**Insight.** Setting aside an allotted time to worry is teaching your brain to be more organised. It's like saying, "Okay, brain, now's the time to worry, but later we have other work to do". This helps us because our brain starts to get better at concentrating on tasks when it's not worry time, almost like we're training it to switch between "worry mode" and "focus mode". By deciding when we worry, we're not only taking back control of our time but also building a skill that makes us stronger emotionally. The key, as always, is doing it regularly.

### Case Study: Light Through the Window

My client Jane was absolutely killing it in her professional life. However, when the office lights were switched off, she was left grappling with a struggle faced by many single people I've met over the years; the societal expectations around getting married and having children. Despite all her career accomplishments she often felt the nagging pressure of her biological clock ticking away, causing her to question her achievements.

Jane found herself stuck in a cycle of thoughts, where memories of relationships played on repeat in her mind like scenes from a movie. She couldn't shake off the worry about a future without a partner or children, and this constant negativity was taking away the happiness and vitality that once fuelled her interactions and interests.

Desperate to break out of this perpetual loop, she reluctantly decided to give the Worry Window a try. Whenever a pessimistic thought arose, she would jot it down and save it for her designated Worry Window time slot. It was, of course, by no means an easy task; at first, it seemed as elusive as trying to catch smoke. Nevertheless, Jane persisted, motivated by her longing to take control of her life from the grip of anxiety. She even enlisted a check-in buddy to hold her accountable because on her own it sometimes felt too hard and heavy.

Her Worry Window sessions gradually transformed into deep dives into her anxieties, uncovering their roots in family and societal pressures as well as her own self-doubts. As Jane started looking at her thoughts from this perspective, and through our work, she learned to distinguish between what was real and what was simply a product of fear that she had inherited from those around her.

As weeks turned into months, Jane realised that her worries about not having children didn't immobilise her as they once did. She came to understand that while she couldn't control every aspect of her life, she could definitely control how she responded to those uncontrollable parts. Rather than viewing these fears as anchors dragging her down, Jane chose to sever the ties that bound her to despair. She knew all too well by now that her fears had expanded into her reality and she was determined to shift that fear into creating a version of herself she felt more in harmony with.

Worry Window gifted Jane with a critical life skill. The ability to guide her thoughts instead of letting them dominate her. This newfound mastery revitalised her outlook on life, allowing for a deeper involvement in the interests that once gave her joy and a rekindled connection with her friends, free from the heavy burden of past anxieties.

Sure, she still dreams of meeting someone and building a family. These dreams no longer consume her. With the space created, she now resides more peacefully in the present, buoyed instead by optimism for the future's possibilities.

Worry Window wasn't a magic pill that instantaneously dissolved Jane's worries. Rather, her story is a reminder of the inner strength we all possess to reshape our mental landscape. It celebrates the diligent, at times challenging, endeavour to engage with our thoughts proactively, steering them towards healthier shores instead of being capsized by them.

# 15

# Art Critic Method: An Artful Approach to Self-Criticism

**Figure 15.1   Artful Self-Insight**

**When to Use.** Whenever you find yourself engaging in self-criticism.

We've all been caught tangled up in the dense underbrush of self-criticism at one time or another. But imagine if you could take a step back and view your thoughts from another perspective. The *Art Critic* method offers a refreshing approach that quite literally takes the "self" out of self-help. This technique blends aspects of neuroscience, philosophy, and a generous dose of creativity.

The foundation of this technique is centred on the concept of *cognitive distancing*, which you can think of as a kind of mental out-of-body experience. So, picture yourself standing in an art gallery. However, in this mental gallery, you take on the dual role of both an observer and the critic, examining each thought as if it were a work of art. No, it's not like those high school literature classes where you go on a search for hidden meanings. Rather, it's about assessing the value of your thoughts and grasping how they're impacting your life without getting trapped in their emotional undercurrent.

There are so many research studies that highlight our brain's capacity to adjust and reorganise itself via techniques such as detachment. These exercises support the creation of neural pathways focused on building emotional strength. Essentially, by taking a step back and observing your thoughts, you train your brain to become better at managing negativity and stress through detachment and objectivity.

I see this approach as being heavily influenced by the Japanese philosophy of *wabi-sabi*, which values imperfections and acknowledges the natural cycle from growth to decline.

> **Wabi-sabi** *is a Japanese aesthetic and philosophy that embraces the beauty of imperfection, transience, and simplicity. It's a worldview that values the natural world and recognises that everything is imperfect, impermanent, and incomplete. Wabi-sabi is characterised by humility, restraint, naturalism, and asymmetry.*[1]

The Art Critic method embraces this ethos when dealing with your thoughts. Instead of striving for a detached position, it invites you

---

[1] Oxford English Dictionary (2021). https://www.oed.com/dictionary/wabi-sabi_adj?tl=true.

to recognise and embrace the imperfect and fleeting nature of your thoughts. This viewpoint doesn't just critique, it also appreciates your perspectives, encouraging you to see your negative thoughts as essential aspects of being human.

But make no mistake, this isn't just another tool for navel-gazing. It's a dynamic strategy for flipping self-criticism on its head, transforming it into a lever for personal evolution and betterment. Aiming to cultivate a kinder relationship with oneself, this method offers a thought-by-thought critique that's anything but dull. It offers an engaging exploration of the inner self unburdened by clichés and filled with genuine curiosity.

## Guide: Applying the Art Critic Method

When you borrow the observation skills of an art critic and use them to analyse your thoughts, you not only change how you see things but also come to value the intricate patterns of your inner world. You can apply it using the following five steps.

### Step 1: Plan Your Gallery Visit

First and foremost, choose a time to visit your gallery. Pick a moment in the morning or a relaxing period before bedtime. Like planning a trip to an art gallery, set aside this time for yourself—a rendezvous with your thoughts that you can't afford to miss.

### Step 2: Curate Your Display

Begin by pinpointing the recurring themes that hold sway over your thoughts. These are the pieces you will be examining closely today— the masterpieces that will be under review. Note them down if it helps. Just as a curator of art carefully selects artworks that evoke certain feelings or tell a story, choose the thoughts currently impacting you the most.

### Step 3: Take on the Role as Observer

Visualise yourself stepping into your personal art gallery, strolling through its corridors and encountering each troublesome thought displayed on a canvas. Observe each of these thoughts one by one without getting emotionally involved. Your purpose is not to change the displayed artwork but to grasp and admire their structure and how they blend harmoniously in your mind. Remember this guiding phrase: "I am here to observe, not interfere".

### Step 4: Critique Each Piece

This isn't an invitation to go ahead and criticise yourself. Critiquing here is driven by curiosity rather than judgement, so it could look something like: "That is a very interesting thought, why is it that I think (or feel) this way?" and "What is this thought trying to teach me?" The answers might not come straight away but at least you are beginning to plant the seeds, knowing they'll reveal themselves when they are ready. Remember, the act of cognitive distancing strengthens your mind's capacity for emotional resilience. You're sculpting your brain's architecture to favour a more balanced mental ecosystem.

Drawing inspiration from the concept of wabi-sabi, we remember that our thoughts are fleeting, they come and go and change over time. Recognising this impermanence can shift your viewpoint, helping you find beauty in the fluctuations of your mind versus getting stuck in the details of them.

### Step 5: Decide on the Fate of Each Exhibit

Now comes the moment to determine which thoughts warrant a permanent display and which should be stored away. Consider reinterpreting some thoughts or viewing them in a new context, while others may no longer merit space in your evolving gallery. This is your gallery; you are in control of the curation. This technique is a constructive process which helps you separate self-criticism from your self-worth.

Exploring the mental gallery with practical phrases like "I wonder what's the story behind this thought?" and "How is this thought helping me get to where I want to be?" helps deepen your independent analysis. You're effectively converting the process of self-examination from a potential quagmire of negativity into an enriching critique designed to help cultivate a more nuanced and resilient inner narrative.

**Insight.**   When you adopt the viewpoint of an observer through the Art Critic method it can help alleviate the intensity of your thoughts. It's fascinating to observe how psychology and neuroscience intersect in this context. By stepping back and considering your thoughts as tangible objects, you activate specific regions of the brain associated with self-regulation and emotional detachment. This detachment can help break the cycle of rumination and intense emotional responses that accompany habitual thought processes. It serves to diminish their influence and dominance over your emotions.

As we conclude our exploration of the Art Critic, remember that when you approach viewing your internal dialogue with the discerning eye of an art critic, you open the door to a more compassionate understanding of yourself. This method encourages self-compassion and patience, allowing you to view your imperfections not as flaws, but as unique brushstrokes that add depth to your personal narrative. Now, let's prepare to dive into the next compelling topic: Re-engage with Your Big "Why". Chapter 16 will guide you in rediscovering your core motivations and purpose—key elements that serve as a powerful antidote to negativity—and help steer your journey towards fulfilment and resilience.

# 16 | Re-engage with Your Big "Why"

**Figure 16.1  Your "Why" Matters**

**When to Use.**  When negativity clouds your motivation or direction.

I've taken inspiration from Aristotle's life teachings, specifically, introducing the world to the concept of *eudaimonia*, which essentially means flourishing and achieving your potential. Aristotle emphasised the importance of discovering your purpose, or nowadays what is often referred to as your "Why", as the key to fulfilment. In embracing this mindset, every obstacle or critique you face becomes an opportunity for growth.

> Eudaimonia *is an ancient Greek word that is often translated as "happiness" or "a good life". In Aristotelianism, eudaimonia is a life of activity that is governed by reason and lived in accordance with one's virtues.*[1]

This shift helps you stay focused and resilient because you know where you're headed, and you can steer those negative thoughts towards actionable steps that align with your real-world goals. Don't get me wrong, you will still of course face difficulties, but adopting this perspective can help you remain undeterred because you can see the right way through them towards your desired direction of travel, which is held crystal clear in your mind's eye.

Nowadays, neuroscience adds another dimension to Aristotle's ideas. Inside our brains lies the *reticular activating system* (RAS), and part of its role is to act as a filter zeroing in on specific information while ignoring irrelevant background noise, helping you focus.[2] When you have a sense of your purpose, the RAS can direct its attention towards people, information and opportunities that can help you achieve them, diminishing negative influences. This process helps maintain your attention on what's genuinely important to you, making the law of attraction appear less mystical. The synergy between these ancient teachings and modern scientific discoveries is clearly demonstrated in how you apply your purpose to everyday life. It's not about retreating into solitude to ponder life's

[1] Duignan, B. (2024). *Britannica*. https://www.britannica.com/topic/eudaimonia.

[2] McAlonan, K., Brown, V.J., and Bowman, E.M. (2000). Thalamic reticular nucleus activation reflects attentional gating during classical conditioning. *Journal of Neuroscience* 20(23): 8897–8901. doi: 10.1523/JNEUROSCI.20-23-08897.2000.

big questions, but about charging right into the fray with intention. Injecting your "Why" into daily tasks elevates them from mundane to meaningful, turning them into steps where each piece aligns with your broader vision. Such continuous alignment serves as an armour against negativity and catapults you towards personal triumph and satisfaction.

Amid your busyness, it's all too easy to focus on the "what" and "how". However, understanding your "Why" serves as a grounding force. For the many professionals I have spoken with, their motivation has revolved around everything from leaving a lasting legacy, obtaining financial stability or freedom, to bringing about positive change in themselves or their chosen endeavour.

My driving force lies in empowering individuals to uncover clarity and healing in their journeys. I find fulfilment in those moments when a client experiences a newfound strength or perspective. It goes beyond appointments and timetables; it's about changing lives one conversation at a time.

Ultimately, knowing your "Why" can give you both stability and direction. It acts as a grounding force when the sea of negativity tries to toss you around; it acts as your compass keeping you moving in the direction you want to go. This amalgamation of timeless philosophical thought and contemporary neurological discovery offers more than just a pep talk; it provides a pragmatic blueprint for a life marked by clarity, achievement, and unwavering optimism, regardless of the obstacles that lie in wait.

For those of you starting out on the path to discovering your "Why", a good place to begin is with those moments that genuinely make you happy or completely absorb your attention, because they serve as subtle clues guiding you forward. Equally important is paying attention to what others admire in you. The qualities appreciated by others can often illuminate your own value and purpose, providing a mirror to see yourself in a new light (as discussed in Chapter 4).

## Guide: Reconnecting to Your "Why"

Getting through your day with a focus on your objectives, skilfully pushing aside that pesky negative voice, is easier said than done. I quite agree. But it doesn't need to be just a utopian dream. The following sections provide a simple four-step guide that can help you stay on track and cultivate a purpose-driven approach to all that you do.

### Step 1: Compress Your "Why" in a Tweet

Can you boil down your purpose into 280 characters or less? This exercise forces you to have clarity and brevity, making your "Why" easy to remember and reflect upon. I suppose you could think of it as your personal slogan, easy to recall during your hectic day. If you're still figuring things out, a sample tweet could be something like:"Each day is a step towards discovering what drives me. Open to change, guided by values".

### Step 2: Infuse Your Purpose into Your Passwords

Here's something you perhaps haven't thought of—use your pass-words as daily reminders of your "Why". Modify your usual passwords to include hints or abbreviations of your purpose. For instance, if empowerment is your goal, your password might become "Empow3r!". It's a really simple, yet effective way to continuously be reinforcing your intentions.

### Step 3: The "Why" Visualisation Break

When you find yourself doing something on autopilot, such as check-ing your phone or going to the supermarket, take a moment for a quick visualisation drill—why not even put it as your phone screen-saver? Envision yourself achieving a milestone that truly resonates with your "Why" and relishing every aspect of that success. Interestingly, science shows that visualisation activates the same brain areas as physi-cally engaging in a task does, thereby strengthening your sense of purpose on a neurological level.

But if you still need some convincing then you might be inter-ested in an intriguing study where two groups of pianists were observed: one group played pieces of music on a piano, while the other only visualised playing these pieces, without physically touch-ing the instrument. Remarkably, brain scans revealed that both groups activated similar areas of the brain, particularly those involved in fine motor skills and musical processing. This suggests that the act of mental visualisation can engage the brain in ways comparable to actual performing.[3]

Now what this means for you is that by taking moments in your day to vividly imagine reaching your goals, you're actually getting your brain involved in a way that reflects real-life action and accomplishment. These quick visualisation practices can act as reinforcement of your goals, essentially teaching your brain to sync up better with your dreams even when you're not actively pursuing them physically.

### Step 4: Inject Practical Positivity into Every Challenge

Think of this step as more than a dash of positivity; see it as a strategic move. When you embrace this perspective, you're essentially programming the RAS in your brain to filter out negativity and highlight the opportunities that drive you closer towards your vision.

When life inevitably sends that curveball your way, how about pausing for a moment to reconsider your viewpoint? Ask yourself, "How does this situation inch me closer to my 'Why'?" For instance, say your project hits a setback; reframe this by telling yourself: "Ah, this is an unexpected chance to stop, reflect, and ensure we're on the most aligned path to our core objectives". This, of course, can help in manoeuvring around obstacles but also turns them into meaningful milestones. You're employing foresight to turn challenges into launching pads of opportunities, much like turning lemons into lemonade, but with a twist of strategic planning!

**Insight.** Infusing your "Why" into your routines taps into a fascinating neuroscientific concept known as Hebb's Law, which suggests that "neurons that fire together wire together".[4] Imagine the everyday acts like entering a password, going to the grocery store, and even confronting daily challenges, being connected to your deeper sense of purpose. Basically, you are constructing a superhighway in your brain, where each repetition strengthens this newfound bond.

---

[3] Bernardi, N.F., De Buglio, M., Trimarchi, P.D. et al. (2013). Mental practice promotes motor anticipation: Evidence from skilled music performance. *Frontiers in Human Neuroscience* 7: 451. doi: 10.3389/fnhum.2013.00451.

[4] Hebb, D.O. (1949). *The Organization of Behavior: A Neuropsychological Theory.* New York: Wiley. https://www.ncbi.nlm.nih.gov/pmc/articles/PMC8284127/.

The outcome? These everyday moments, and your overarching "Why", begin to harmonise subtly, guiding your behaviours towards aligning with your objectives. It's like turning your brain into a purpose-focused GPS, realigning your day-to-day activities with the bigger picture that's in your mind.

In conclusion, reflecting on your greater purpose means aligning what you do with what you value and your future aspirations. This reflective process not only reaffirms your reason for being but also bolsters your dedication to chasing what is genuinely important to you. Make sure that every move you make is guided by understanding and purpose. As you'll see next in Chapter 17, we explore how to find tranquillity at night, which is often when those pesky negative thoughts run rampant. Calming them down and maintaining a more peaceful mind allows you to continue pursuing your goals with renewed vigour and focus.

# 17 | Mind Mute: Make Peace with the Night

**Figure 17.1   Mute Your Mind at Night**

**When to Use.**   When the lights go out and your thoughts start to spiral, hit *Mind Mute* to silence them.

There really is a special kind of frustration that occurs when you're all set to drift off to sleep and bam—your thoughts decide to sprint off in the opposite direction. This all too common experience is linked to the complex science behind sleep and how our brains operate during night-time. More specifically, as we start to unwind, the part of our brain responsible for decision-making and problem-solving, known as the prefrontal cortex, becomes unusually active. It's as though our mind just can't resist the quiet of the night and takes full advantage by going into overdrive—perhaps ruminating over mishaps of the day, feeling overstimulated by too much screen time or intense conversations right before bedtime, or fretting about what lies ahead. These are some of the many culprits contributing to the night-time chaos. Meanwhile, the poor pineal gland, which is essential for regulating sleep by producing melatonin, struggles to send strong enough signals that it can override the cortex's heightened busyness.

At this point, I'd better just mention that this explanation is somewhat overly simplified. Actually, the relationship between brain activity and sleep is also heavily influenced by many other elements, such as exposure to internal circadian rhythms and individual reactions to stress. When all these factors come together, coupled with the battle between a racing mind and the body's urge for rest, it can lead to nights of tossing and turning as we strive for sleep.

In light of this understanding, the difficulties with traditional sleep aids become more apparent for those of you who find your mind racing even when your body longs for rest. This is where the Mind Mute technique comes into play, offering a perspective that particularly resonates with minds, like mine, that struggle with intrusive thoughts at bedtime. Instead of trying to silence or reason with these thoughts, which can feel impossible even at the best of times, *Mind Mute* suggests gently guiding the mind away from daily worries towards a state of tranquillity at night-time, ensuring that sleep isn't just a possibility but a certainty. By following this approach, you send a clear message to your brain that night-time is for dreaming, not for debates.

## Guide: Applying the Mind Mute Tool

Let's now take a look at a five-step approach to how you can seamlessly integrate the Mind Mute method into your nightly routine.

### Step 1: CTRL-Shift-Redirect

Just as a cowboy throws a lasso around his target, when you feel your mind racing as you attempt to relax it's important to take control of that moment. This signals to your brain a calling for a change in direction. Recognising this increase in mental activity is the first move to guide your mind towards a state of calmness.

### Step 2: Set the Stage

Make sure that your nightstand has tranquillity tools for relaxation, such as a notebook, pen, a basic alarm clock, leaving any electronic devices in another room. Having these essentials in place again signals to your brain that you are now beginning a soothing routine. Think of it like preparing for a play; once everything is in place the performance (or, in this instance, winding down) can proceed more smoothly.

### Step 3: Capture and Release

Now for the tricky part. When a thought bubbles to the surface, which let's face it doesn't usually take too long, make a note of it without interacting with it. You could think of it as catching butterflies, gently tagging them and then releasing them without hurting or holding onto them for long. This practice employs the brain's executive functions, redirecting your focus and energy away from rumination and overthinking to taking action towards paving the way for a more peaceful transition into relaxation. Expressing the thoughts out of your head and onto paper also activates several regions of the brain, including the hippocampus, which plays a role in memory. This can be especially active when reflecting on personal thoughts, so jotting them down signifies that you are in control and that this thought will be revisited but at a better time for you.

### Step 4: Set the Stage for Tomorrow

For every troublesome thought you jot down, tell yourself something like: "This needs attention and I will revisit it just after breakfast". This simple reminder helps ease the pressure of thoughts that might linger in your mind and disrupt your sleep. By deciding to tackle these thoughts at a dedicated time, you're letting your brain know that they are important but can wait for a more convenient moment to be addressed. Don't forget to review your list the following morning to solidify trust in this practice.

### Step 5: Close the Loop

Every time you jot down a thought and set a reminder to circle back to it later, you're essentially closing a mental loop in your brain. This concept is known as the Zeigarnik effect (covered in Chapter 6), in which tasks that have been completed are less likely to remain active in our memory. It tells your brain that it's okay to let go of the thought for now, thereby closing the loop and making it easier to drift into sleep.

**Insight.**   Writing down your thoughts regularly just before bedtime can make a difference in how your mind behaves as you prepare to sleep. Initially, your thoughts may still be racing, however, if you continue this practice something interesting happens. Your brain begins to understand that these thoughts will be addressed at some point, just not immediately. Over time you'll observe intervals between the thoughts as your brain naturally adopts a more organised approach to bedtime. This routine not only enhances sleep quality but also demonstrates how small consistent actions can lead to transformations in your thought patterns.

### Case Study: How COO John Found Rest in the Rush

John's story goes well beyond conquering insomnia; it embodies perseverance amidst unrelenting work demands. Serving as the Chief Operating Officer (COO) of a growing tech firm and leading a team of 400 wasn't a role—it was an around-the-clock dedication that literally seeped into every facet of his life, most especially affecting his sleep.

When John sought my help, he was teetering on the edge of despair, yearning for a moment of peace during the night. This led us to explore the Mind Mute technique as part of his journey. Initially, John was hesitant. "How could simply jotting down thoughts really aid my sleep?" he asked sceptically, quickly followed by, "Surely Jay that would keep me awake even longer?" Despite his doubts and the fact that he was already awake a lot longer than he wanted to be, his intense fatigue and desperation for a restful night compelled him to give it a shot.

The initial phase was far from easy. Every evening when he settled in to pour out his thoughts onto paper he struggled. Some nights seemed hopeless because even after jotting everything down his mind kept churning away, leaving him gazing at the ceiling and questioning if things would ever improve.

Nevertheless, he kept at it as a nightly ritual more than anything else and then the tide began to turn. Gradually, John started noticing brief glimmers of quietness in his mind after writing in his notebook. It didn't happen instantly, and it certainly wasn't constant, but it was happening. This shift wasn't only in his thoughts; it seemed physical somehow. Writing down his feelings was easing the weight he was carrying on his mind bit by bit.

Yet, it was a journey punctuated with obstacles. Just as John believed he had started to figure out how to get a grip on switching off and relaxing, a critical project or a fast-tracked deadline would land in his lap, causing his stress hormones to spike, making his recent coping method appear futile. It was during these times that John's determination faced a challenge all of its own. Instead of giving in to irritation, he adapted by integrating the Balloon Strategy exercise (explained in Chapter 12), putting uncontrollable thoughts into a metaphorical balloon and watching them float away, into his nightly writing routine. These changes were not last-minute efforts, they were strategies to regain authority over his restless thoughts.

The real testament to John's progress came not from the peaceful nights of sleep but from the difficult nights. On these nights, when he felt the strategy was letting him down, John didn't revert to his old ways of tossing and turning in despair. Instead, he remained committed to doubling down on his efforts to stick with it. All the while he reminded himself that change is often a series of ebbs and flows and that what was happening was almost less important than who he was becoming in the process.

As time passed it became increasingly clear that John's dedication was making an impact. The mornings took on a sense of vitality, with less grogginess and more rejuvenation. His colleagues began to observe a change in his attitude; the once stressed-out COO now appeared more approachable and composed.

Are you, like John, trapped in what feels like an endless cycle of sleepless nights caused by work-related stress? If so, this approach emphasises a simple but potent message; the path to a peaceful state of mind is filled with endless obstacles and hurdles. However, it is only through perseverance, flexibility, and the right strategies for you that achieving serenity in the chaos becomes attainable. The Mind Mute technique—though simple in concept—proved to be a lifeline for John, improving not just his nights but also his days.

# PART

# VII | Self-Confidence

I'm sure you've noticed those individuals who have this enchanting ability to finalise a deal with finesse, give an Oscar-worthy presentation, or effortlessly charm an audience, simply by radiating an unshakeable air of self-confidence. It's almost like they possess some sort of secret superpower.

Well, contrary to popular opinion, and much to my own relief, confidence isn't this mystical and magical gift bestowed upon a select fortunate few from birth. It's actually a skill that can be developed, rooted in brain science and with knowledge that if leveraged, can rewire our thinking habits. It's available to anyone ready to invest the effort.

An easy way to understand confidence is to think of it as a muscle. Similar to any other muscle in your body, it gets stronger through repetition and regular practice. Many exciting studies have shed light on how confidence operates in the brain. Research using fMRI scans reveals that when you exude confidence the prefrontal cortex region of your brain, responsible for decision-making, becomes highly active, which helps you when you're navigating complex situations and to contemplate and make decisions with more clarity and conviction.[1]

---

[1] Bang, D., Moran, R., Daw, N.D. et al. (2022). Neurocomputational mechanisms of confidence in self and others. *Nature Communications* 13: 4238. doi: 10.1038/s41467-022-31674-w.

However, that's only the beginning. Scientists have also pointed out the role of neurotransmitters, such as dopamine and serotonin, in developing and sustaining self-assurance. Dopamine, known as the "reward chemical", not only brings about feel-good feelings from taking confident actions but also reinforces them by establishing a cycle of positive reinforcement in your brain, motivating you to replicate the behaviours that led to your success.[2] Conversely, serotonin is a "mood chemical" associated with feelings of contentment and joy that can be increased through simple practices like maintaining good posture, engaging in meaningful interactions, or volunteering and supporting others.[3]

It is also fascinating to learn about the influence of *mirror neurons*. These uniquely specialised brain cells are not only active when you take action but also when you observe others doing the same action. If you think about it, simply being around confident people could enhance your confidence by triggering these mirror neurons and prompting similar behavioural responses in your brain. If you have ever read *The 7 Habits of Highly Effective People*, by Stephen Covey, you'll understand the significance of being around people who radiate positive energy.

In this section, we'll explore quick and simple strategies to build unwavering self-assurance with techniques that are backed by science and, as always, designed to integrate into busy schedules.

---

[2] Schultz, W. (2015). Neuronal reward and decision signals: From theories to data. *Physiological Reviews* 95(3): 853–951. doi: 10.1152/physrev.00023.2014.
[3] Watson, S. (2023). Serotonin: The natural mood booster. *Harvard Health*. Available at: https://www.health.harvard.edu/mind-and-mood/serotonin-the-natural-mood-booster.

# 18

# Fast-Track Your Confidence

**Figure 18.1   Fast-Track Your Confidence**

**When to Use.**   Whenever your pep talks just aren't cutting it.

When it comes to self-confidence, words matter immensely. We often hear the phrase "actions speak louder than words", but let us not forget they are certainly not a replacement for them. A spoken word has immense power because your words reflect your reputation, personality, and character. Take a moment to reflect on your recent conversations and consider: What do your words reveal about you?

Perhaps you feel proud of how you engage with the people around you. But how about the recent conversations you've had with yourself? Now, I can't say my self-talk is quite so kind. Nevertheless, I always find it a relief to acknowledge that we cannot create anything of value without first experiencing feelings of both self-doubt and self-belief. Without self-doubt, it's easy to become complacent, and of course, without self-belief, you cannot succeed, you really do need both.

I want to share a line from a beautiful poem by Mary Oliver that I often reflect upon during my moments of insecurity:

> Whoever you are, no matter how lonely,
> the world offers itself to your imagination.[1]

Whenever I fall into the trap of competition or self-doubt, I think about literature and the many experimental novels that do not follow the traditional form. It can be lonely daring to follow a road less travelled, but my story, much like yours, isn't traditional, and each day is **my** day.

## Quick Wins for the Time-Starved

But, as you know, I'm not here just to offer a motivational pep talk, so let's talk strategies. Now, like with everything else, some strategies demand a deep dive into your psyche, while others are quick and can fit seamlessly into your busy schedule. In this section, we will focus on the latter. I'm all about those bite-sized tools that can pack a punch. I've cherry-picked 18 of the simplest and cleverest practical pivots that can transform how you carry yourself and others see you, inspired by communication experts such as Dale Carnegie, Mel Robbins, and Jefferson Fisher.

---

[1] Oliver, M. (1986). *Dream Work*. New York: Atlantic Monthly Press.

## 1. Avoid Using Verbal Placeholders

By this, I mean "Umm", or "Uh…" I appreciate that it's unintentional, but you're undermining your sentence before it has even begun. Instead, keep it really simple and begin with taking a breath as if that were your first word. Take a moment to breathe in and out and then respond. This momentary silence can often be more powerful than filler words because it reflects a more thoughtful and measured communication.

The tone used is equally important, so aim to use the same tone you would use when you say something matter of fact, like "Please close the door". Apply this assured tone to all your requests and statements to eliminate any uncertainty in your voice. So, for example, replace: "I can get this report to you by Tuesday?" (notice the upward inflexion at the end whenever you ask a question), with a more assured: "I can get it to you by Monday".

## 2. Stand Up for Yourself

The first thing to know about confidently standing up for yourself is knowing when it's necessary. Just because someone speaks negatively to you doesn't mean they are automatically worthy of your attention, so there is no need to stand up for yourself to everyone who crosses you. Can you imagine if Superman stopped every single jaywalker in Metropolis? That would be exhausting work and, let's face it, a bit of an overkill. Similarly, not every situation requires a showdown.

However, when you do need to stand up and step into the spotlight it's important not to automatically begin with an apology (out of habit) or use uncertain language. For example, it's not: "I'm sorry but I'm kind of feeling uncomfortable about this"; it's "I feel uncomfortable". Be clear in expressing your feelings and boundaries without feeling the need to apologise.

It's always helpful to practise important phrases you often struggle with, like saying "no", without providing justifications. If you start justifying your decisions the other person may focus on trying to argue against your reasoning, instead of keeping their focus on finding a solution. I always recommend that whenever dealing with someone particularly difficult, it is worth skipping the formalities and keeping it short and sweet; that is, factual and polite.

### 3. Assert Your Needs Without Using "Sorry"

"Sorry" to harp on about this, but how many times have you, or someone around you, initiated a request with "sorry"? "Sorry to bother you but can I ask a quick question", "Sorry I haven't got around to this yet". Over-apologising in this way diminishes your self-worth and authority because essentially what you're really doing in those little "sorry" moments is tapping into a deep-seated need for approval, acceptance, or avoiding conflict.

It's time to realise that your worth is not tied to how little of an inconvenience you can be whenever you need something from somebody. Simply state what you need without the apology, for instance, "Could I have a moment of your time when you're available", or "I appreciate your patience". By asserting your needs there's no need for an apology. Similarly, you can replace "sorry" with a "thank you" when required, for instance, "thank you for your time", or "thank you for your patience". Save your "sorry" for when you truly need to apologise.

### 4. Be Unfazed When Someone Doesn't Like You

If someone doesn't seem to like you, I advise treating them as if they do (yes, you read that correctly). Being distant or cold back at them only gives them the power to influence your feelings. Remember, if they don't like you that is their opinion and shouldn't bear any weight over how you carry yourself. Also, there is a high probability that if they don't like you, they're not that important, so don't let somebody else affect your mood and take away the best parts of your personality.

It can be helpful, however, when having to converse with such a person to stick to neutral facts and stay away from the emotional, because when you do that, it's like you're on a mission, you have an objective and your purpose is clear. For example, you might say: "I'm here because I'm required to have your input on the proposal", and you keep the conversation brief to avoid any misunderstanding or negativity. Better still, put a conversation limit on the topic because the longer you talk the more opportunity you have for it to nose dive into negativity.

### 5. Get Comfortable in Small Talk

Making small talk isn't everyone's cup of tea, myself included. Nevertheless, it's worth having a couple of questions up your sleeve for those inevitable moments. I like to try and steer clear from static questions like "How was your weekend", which often elicit a closed-ended response like "Yeah good". Instead, try to make the questions you ask more action-oriented, for example, "What was the highlight of your weekend?", which opens up the conversation making it much more interesting. Another Friday favourite people like to ask is "Do you have any weekend plans?", which can limit the response to yes or no. Try instead, "Where're you off to this weekend?" Potentially sparking a more lively discussion.

However, if you find yourself struggling for things to talk about it might also be a sign that your interest in the conversation is waning. It's okay to end the chat, rather than forcing it and letting the other person sense your disinterest. Plan ahead with some phrases to politely eject yourself, for instance, "It was nice talking to you. I need to go now but let's touch base again soon".

Having these kinds of pre-rehearsed sentence structures in place can help make social interactions more manageable, promote assertiveness, improve communication, and, above all, contribute to building confidence.

### 6. Avoid Words That Clog Your Sentences

"Like" is one word that really clogs up sentences and a much better substitute is to use "because" or a different conjunction that helps your sentences flow better and helps convey your message. For instance, if I were to say "I resent you saying that, like it made me feel unappreciated", it may sound less impactful compared to saying "I resent you saying that because it made me unappreciated".

Other words you might want to try dropping from the end of your sentences are "you know", "so", "anyway", and so forth that leave your sentence incomplete, and instead replace them with a period, which denotes an end rather than leaving your sentences hanging. For example, instead of saying "I know that my experience justifies a higher position so…" replace with a more firm, "I know that my experience justifies a higher position". But if you do struggle to catch yourself, inform those close to you who can support and hold you accountable. It might feel awkward at first, but I've always found that speaking slowly and getting comfortable in creating dead space, instead of filler words, in sentences helps in sounding more confident.

### 7. Stay Confident When Someone Is Condescending

Instead of accepting their bad behaviour or reacting negatively, both of which keep you in an inferior position, you can assert yourself by letting them know that their words are beneath your standards. For example, "Your words are under the threshold of what I find acceptable". By shifting the power dynamic in this way, you take control of the situation.

You can help them out by encouraging them to adjust their approach. Using language like "I want to allow you an opportunity to communicate differently" sends a very clear message that you are in control of how you wish to be treated. It's also helpful to set expectations by stating what you are willing to engage in, such as having a conversation only if mutual respect or a calm demeanour is maintained. This approach guides the conversation towards a respectful interaction.

### 8. Take Control of the Conversation When You're Upset

You can confidently take the lead in the conversation by setting the tone and strategic direction. For example, "I'd like to talk about your comments in yesterday's meeting". Then guide the conversation towards your desired outcome, which you can do by expressing your intentions and seeking agreement from the other person. For instance, you could say: "I'd like to discuss what was said with the aim of improving communication between us. Does that work for you?" When you frame a conversation in this way it will rarely result in them saying "no".

### 9. Respond to Contempt with Confidence and Poise

If someone disrespects you, I know this might be challenging but silently and slowly count to ten (in your head) after they finish speaking. This will give them just enough time to reflect back on what they just said to you. By not reacting as expected, you show control. Then politely express that their behaviour doesn't meet your standards of respect and response. Let them know that your values are higher than what they displayed, which is shifting the power dynamic. Remember that whatever they say in return won't in any way match the strength of your message. Always stand firm by your principles when faced with disrespect.

## 10. Rise Above Taking Personal Offence

If you tend to take things personally you might end up holding onto issues that were never meant for you in the first place. This can create a self-fulfilling prophecy where your ego convinces you that someone else's actions were specifically negatively aimed at you.

This negative belief then transforms into your perceived truth. In my line of work, I find it helpful to remind myself to "let go" of other people's stuff by saying the phrase "Jay, it's not your poison to carry" whenever I start taking things personally. When I manage to do this, I notice an increase in my self-confidence and peace of mind. There's something incredibly healing about developing this habit that makes me more inclined to be generous in giving others the benefit of the doubt.

## 11. Respond to Questions with Confidence

When it comes to answering questions with confidence it's pretty simple when you know how. Try switching up words like "I think" or "I believe" with "I'm confident". So, imagine being in a job interview and tackling questions by replacing "I believe that my experience is well suited to this role" with "I'm confident my experience is well suited to this role". This change works because using the words "I'm confident" reinforces that quality in the interviewer's mind.

Now let's talk about dropping the phrase "does that make sense?" from your responses. Here you are subtly conveying that perhaps what you have said is either unclear or lacks clarity and is moving more towards seeking affirmation that you were understood. You could instead say "What are your thoughts?" or "I'd love to hear your input on this", which is more self-assured and encourages a two-way dialogue. And rather than expressing uncertainty in your responses by saying "I'm not sure", you could rephrase as "Oh, I haven't come across that yet", which I use all the time!

In using these alternatives you're demonstrating more ownership of your words as well as confidence in your ability to convey your ideas effectively.

## 12. Ask for Help

When seeking assistance it's important to be clear from the start and make it personal too, so instead of just saying "Can you help me?", you could replace it with "I'd value your input on tomorrow's agenda" or "I could use your creativity in my proposal". By tailoring your request to someone's strengths they are more likely to lend a hand.

Also, avoid downplaying your need for help by eliminating phrases like "I hate to ask but…". A personal pet peeve of mine is "This might be a stupid question but…". Confident people don't pretend to know everything and acknowledge when they require assistance without the need for apologies or self-deprecation. As always, if you do struggle with asking for help, try pre-rehearsing an upcoming scenario with a trusted friend, colleague, or family member.

## 13. Avoid Overexplaining Yourself

The tendency to overexplain oneself is something I come across almost daily. It often stems from a fear of not being believed, leading to a tendency to over-provide details in the hope of convincing others of the truth, or knowledge on a subject. However, using too many words can actually make your explanation less believable and further from the truth. Overexplaining doesn't prevent misunderstanding; it practically ensures it.

So, instead of assuming that someone wants to know every single detail and pre-emptively offering up all the information in one hit, try waiting for them to ask questions. Adopting the mindset that if they want to know something they will inquire can help you avoid elaboration.

A useful test to know whether you are guilty of overexplaining is to look at how many times you use the word "because". Consider whether the information is genuinely needed and requested of you, or if you are just assuming its necessity. If it's more about your perception than their requirement, consider omitting it in communication or advising that you are happy to elaborate further if they wish.

### 14. *Handle Insults*

If someone I don't know well insults me for some reason, I would always politely request them to repeat the insult they just made. This often catches them off guard, thereby immediately deflating the intended initial impact of their insult. For instance, I would say "I missed what you said, would you remind repeating it please". When they repeat it, I would very slowly repeat back their words so they have to hear it and then leave it hanging in silence, the intended impact is dramatically diminished—and whatever high they were expecting from my reaction, sadly they wouldn't get it.

In the case where someone I know insults me, I would allow them their opinion as a way to disarm their attempt to put me down by saying "Sure, you are entitled to believe what you believe". By allowing them their insult, I strip away any satisfaction they might have derived from seeing a reaction. Also, I'd then probably take the opportunity to check in and see how they're doing, making it clear that I'm still feeling very much in control.

### 15. *Confront the Elephant in the Room*

This situation can be tricky because you might not even know why the other person is visibly annoyed with you. In this case, you could try to guess their thoughts at that moment. For instance, you could start by suggesting "I am guessing you might be frustrated with the way I handled myself in our earlier discussion". By doing this you're naming the elephant; that is, creating a pathway for them to express their concerns.

Now at this point, the other person has an opportunity to correct any assumptions you have just made. For example, they might respond by clarifying "It's not that I was frustrated, it's just that your tone was dismissive which upset me". People tend to find it easier to correct misconceptions, rather than openly share their feelings. By encouraging them to reveal their concerns without pressure you are better positioned to understand their perspective. This leads to constructive discussions about addressing underlying issues.

### 16. *Rise Above One-Upper's*

Dealing with someone who always tries to one-up you can be frustrating and challenging in equal measure. When they constantly feel the need to outdo your accomplishments it may signal a lack of connection or support. It's important to see this behaviour as a sign that they might not be the person to share your joys and successes with. Instead of getting drawn into a competition, it's okay to let them have their moment.

Responding with neutral comments like "That's nice" or "I'm happy for you" can help maintain boundaries without engaging.

It can also be helpful to look beyond their need to one-up and consider the insecurities driving their behaviour. By understanding where their actions stem from, it becomes easier not to take things personally and avoid getting defensive in response. At the same time, perhaps take a moment to consider why their behaviour bothers you and explore if there's a chance for personal growth.

### 17. Handle Embarrassment

Whenever something embarrassing happens to me, which of course it does, like when I trip over and fall in front of other people, instead of quietly wishing the ground would open up and swallow me whole, I just admit it out loud, saying "Oops, I just fell!" Similarly, if you accidentally call someone by the wrong name, own up to it by saying something like "Sorry about that mix-up!" Speaking out loud about these mishaps helps you acknowledge your feelings and prevents negative emotions from taking control.

It's so important to speak kindly to yourself, and certainly avoid calling yourself stupid or clumsy. Remember that such harsh and critical words only harm yourself. Give yourself the freedom to be human and make mistakes.

I know it's not always easy but I do also try to find humour in my embarrassing moments. Laughing at yourself shows that you don't take things seriously and makes you more likeable and relatable to others. After all, our embarrassing moments often turn into the funniest stories in the end!

### 18. Master Self-Talk

Lastly, you can improve your self-esteem by not always relying on other people's words for your self-worth because sometimes their spoken word, loyalty, or opinions of you can easily be damaged. Instead, focus on aspects you can control, such as how kindly you speak to yourself; work on self-improvement and practise self-forgiveness. My favourite time to practise building the mental muscle of self-affirming thoughts is while waiting in queues or stuck in traffic, whereupon I take a moment to reflect upon the qualities I like about myself, which pleasantly distracts from my impatience while waiting. Remember that self-esteem is not something to seek out but a reflection of what's already within you. Sometimes, the key lies in finding contentment rather than boosting confidence.

As we conclude this chapter, remember to embrace each new day as an opportunity to apply what you've learned, fostering a life filled with resilience, growth, and unapologetic self-assurance.

# 19 | Final Thoughts

And there you have it—a set of tools not designed for the workbench, but for the most marvellous machine you own: your brain. I've explored the messiness of everyday life to arm you with time-tested practical strategies that you can slot into your day to untangle the knotty world of the modern-day professional hustle.

I trust that you now have in your arsenal a Swiss Army knife of your favourite tools, each one ready to spring into action when your mind goes into working overtime. Just remember, wielding these tools isn't about making your life run smoothly; it's about creating little havens of calm amidst those rough and tough moments.

Whether it is finding a way to settle your nerves before a presentation, or developing routines that strengthen your ability to bounce back, you now have a set of tools at your disposal. Use them, pass them along, and most importantly appreciate the journey navigating through the crazy ups and downs of a busy life, knowing that each step is a valuable part of your growth and success. Don't forget to take a screenshot of the visual images accompanying your favourite tools to serve as a quick reminder whenever you need them.

With your beautiful brain constantly changing, it is always eager to pick up skills. Keep stimulating it, keep pushing its limits, and keep giving it the tender loving care it deserves. After all, your brain can be your best friend and ally on this wild, thrilling, coffee-fuelled journey we call a career.

As we now bid our farewells, this isn't goodbye; it's more "see you soon". Here's to living a life with less stress, more zest, and cultivating a wonderfully curious mind. Now, as you go forth and conquer with confidence—remember to always take it one mindful step at a time.

# Index